Top 25 locator map
(continues on inside
back cover)
←

CityPack
Beijing *Top 25*

SEAN SHEEHAN

If you have any comments
or suggestions for this guide
you can contact the editor at
Citypack@theAA.com

AA Publishing
Find out more about AA Publishing and the
wide range of services the AA provides by
visiting *www.theAA.com/bookshop*

About This Book

KEY TO SYMBOLS

➕ Map reference to the accompanying fold-out map and Top 25 locator map

✉ Address

☎ Telephone number

🕐 Opening/closing times

🍴 Restaurant or café on premises or nearby

🚆 Nearest train station

Ⓜ Nearest subway station

🚌 Nearest bus route

🚢 Nearest riverboat or ferry stop

♿ Facilities for visitors with disabilities

✋ Admission charges: Expensive (over 50 yuan), Moderate (20–50 yuan) and Inexpensive (under 20 yuan)

↔ Other nearby places of interest

❓ Other practical information

▶ Indicates the page where you will find a fuller description

ℹ Tourist information

ORGANIZATION

This guide is divided into six chapters:
- Planning Ahead, Getting There
- Living Beijing—Beijing Now, Beijing Then, Time to Shop, Out and About, Walks, Beijing by Night
- Beijing's Top 25 Sights
- Beijing's Best—best of the rest
- Where To—detailed listings of restaurants, hotels, shops and nightlife
- Travel Facts—practical information

In addition, easy-to-read side panels provide extra facts and snippets, highlights of places to visit and invaluable practical advice.

The colors of the tabs on the page corners match the colors of the triangles aligned with the chapter names on the contents page opposite.

MAPS

The fold-out map in the wallet at the back of this book is a comprehensive street plan of Beijing. The first (or only) grid reference given for each attraction refers to this map. **The Top 25 locator map** found on the inside front and back covers of the book itself is for quick reference. It shows the Top 25 Sights, described on pages 26–50, which are clearly plotted by number (**1**–**25**, not page number) across the city. The second map reference given for the Top 25 Sights refers to this map.

Contents

Planning Ahead

WHEN TO GO

It is best to visit Beijing between September and mid-November, when temperatures are pleasant and there is little rain. Everything closes around Chinese New Year (late January or early February)—not a good time to visit. If you don't mind gray skies and snow flurries, December is worth considering as there are few crowds.

TIME

Beijing is 13 hours ahead of New York, 16 hours ahead of Los Angeles and 8 hours ahead of GMT.

AVERAGE DAILY MAXIMUM TEMPERATURES

JAN	FEB	MAR	APR	MAY	JUN	JUL	AUG	SEP	OCT	NOV	DEC
25°F	29°F	40°F	57°F	65°F	76°F	81°F	77°F	64°F	57°F	40°F	23°F
-4°C	-2°C	5°C	14°C	19°C	24°C	27°C	25°C	18°C	14°C	5°C	-5°C
❄	❄	☀	☀	☀	🌧	🌧	🌧	☀	☀	☀	❄

Beijing has four distinct seasons, with extreme temperatures in winter and summer.
Spring (April to May) is dry, with a wind from the Gobi Desert blowing across the city.
Summer (June to August) is uncomfortably hot and very humid.
Fall (September to mid-November) is pleasant, with comfortable temperatures and virtually no rain.
Winter (mid-November to March) sees freezing winds from Siberia, which can cause temperatures to plunge as low as 50°F (-10°C).

WHAT'S ON

January *Spring Festival Concert.*
January/February *Chinese New Year* (on the first day of the first moon): The most important festival in the year. Celebrations are held in the Great Bell Temple (► 28), Ditan Park (► 54) and elsewhere.
February/March *Lantern Festival:* also governed by the lunar cycle. Families celebrate together in the evenings, especially in parks. Lanterns are placed on the ground around picnicking groups.

March/April *Guanyin's Birthday:* a good time to visit the temples. Guanyin is the goddess of mercy.
April *Martial Arts Festival:* martial arts displays at the Great Wall at Badaling (► 29). *Tomb Sweeping Day/Clear Brightness Festival* (5 Apr; 4 Apr in leap years): Relatives pay respects to their ancestors by sweeping their tombs and burning 'ghost money.'
May *May Day* (1 May): International Labor Day is marked by floral displays citywide and celebrations in

Tian'anmen Square. *Youth Day* (4 May).
October *National Day* (1 Oct): The founding of the People's Republic of China is marked by colorful flags, bunting and red lanterns. *Mid-Autumn Festival* (on the 15th day of the eighth moon): Families picnic, gaze at the moon and eat the traditional sweet moon cakes—an acquired taste.
October/November *Beijing Music Festival:* More than 1,000 foreign and home-grown musicians participate in 20 concerts (6593 0250).

BEIJING ONLINE

Suggesting internet sites about China still remains a tricky business. The central government continuously monitors websites, and crackdowns are sporadic and unpredictable, unexpectedly blocking sites. At press time, the following sites are available.

www.beijingpage.com
Everything you need to know about the city, from museums and other attractions, to entertainment, food and drink, and even the weather.

www.thatsbeijing.com
Website of the popular English-language listings magazine. Tells you what artists are in town and where to eat, drink and play sports.

www.btmbeijing.com
The online version of the monthly magazine, *Beijing This Month* is a good up-to-the-minute source for dining and bar listings.

www.chinatravelservice.com
The Hong Kong-based travel agency that serves Beijing and offers details of tours, hotels and sightseeing in Beijing and China as a whole.

http://english.people.com.cn
This is the home page for the Beijing-based English-language daily. It's worth visiting for the state spin on news.

www.scmp.com
The site of the *South China Morning Post*, Hong Kong's English language daily, used to give more balanced accounts of China's news than any mainland publication. However, as it increasingly attempts to gain a market share on the mainland, it is becoming less provocative than it was.

www.tour-beijing.com
This web page of Beijing Xinjua International Tours is a useful source for background information and maps.

GOOD TRAVEL SITES

www.fodors.com
A complete travel-planning site. You can research prices and weather; book air tickets, cars and rooms; pose questions (and get answers) to fellow travelers; and find links to other sites.

www.cits.net
This official state tourism agency offers details on a range of tour packages, as well as some useful China travel tips.

Getting There

INSURANCE

Make sure your policy covers accidents, medical expenses, personal liability, trip cancellation, delayed departure and loss or theft of personal property. In the event of illness or injury requiring treatment, obtain an English translation of documents or receipts written in Chinese.

MONEY

RMB (Renminbi) is the currency of China. The basic unit is the yuan (pronounced 'kuai'), which is made up of 10 jiao (pronounced 'mao'), each of which is again divided into 10 fen. There are notes for 1, 5, 10, 20, 50 and 100 yuan, and the smaller 1, 2 and 5 jiao. There are also coins for 1, 2 and 5 yuan; 1, 2 and 5 jiao; and 1, 2 and 5 fen.

20 yuan

50 yuan

100 yuan

ARRIVING

Capital Airport is 17 miles (27km) northeast of the city center. This is Beijing's only airport and most airlines with flights to China come into Beijing. There are two adjoining terminals for international and domestic flights.

ARRIVING AT CAPITAL AIRPORT

The airport is modern and efficient with cafés and curio shops. Be sure to arrive at least 2 hours in advance when departing; huge Japanese or Chinese tourist groups can clog up the check-in and customs and immigration desks. The rate of airport departure tax is 90 yuan.

The taxi fare into the city is around 100 yuan, cabs are metered—don't try to haggle. The journey takes around 25 minutes, depending on the amount of traffic. Taxi driving is considered safe but not as safe as in London and New York since many new drivers are taking to the roads. Shuttle buses run every 15 minutes, 24 hours a day, between the airport and the city. The fare is 16 yuan, and the journey takes around 30 minutes. Pick up shuttles from the China Aviation Building; drop offs are outside the airport international terminal. The five routes (lines) make stops along the way near big hotels and subway stations. Buy tickets from the airport information desk, where a route leaflet is available, or from the sales point by the buses.

Arriving by Train
There are five railroad stations in Beijing. West Railway Station at Lianhuachi (▓ A8) handles routes to and from the south and west, including Hong Kong (journey time 28 hours).

Arriving by Bus
There are no international bus routes, but the four main stations—Dongzhimen, Haihutun, Yongdingmen and Quianmen—are served by buses to different parts of the country.

Car Rental
Car rental is not recommended.

Customs
Two liters of any alcohol may be imported. You can bring in up to 400 cigarettes or the same amount of tobacco. You can also import up to 50 grams of gold, and up to 20,000 yuan notes. The importation of foreign currency exceeding US$5,000 should be declared. Chinese currency cannot be exported. Special documentation is required for the export of antiques (➤ 72).

Getting Around
The best way to get around is either by the subway or in taxis. The subway runs between 5am and 10.30 or 11pm on two main lines, the main circle line and the east–west line. Four new lines will be operational by 2008. Station names are in English on the platforms and an announcement in English is made on the train as it approaches the station. Buy tickets inside the station from cash desks and show them to the clerk at the top of the subway staircase. Taxis are inexpensive and plentiful. Always ask someone at your hotel to write down your destination in Chinese, and show this to the driver before setting off. Ask your hotel doorman to confirm that the taxi driver knows where you are going. The least expensive taxis are small uncomfortable yellow vans. Stick with regular small-car taxis.
Public buses are often horrendously crowded. For more information on getting around ➤ 90–91.

ENTRY REQUIREMENTS

Visitors must hold a valid passport, with an expiry date at least six months after arrival, and a visa. A single-entry visa is usually valid for 30 days and must generally be used within three months of issue. Visas usually take three to five working days to obtain and are available through your country's Chinese Embassy or consulate and through specialist tour operators. One-month visa extensions can sometimes be arranged through the Public Security Bureau ✉ 2 Andingmen Dongdajie ☎ 6404 7799. No vaccinations are required, but some doctors recommend inoculation against Hepatitis A.

VISITORS WITH DISABILITIES

Little or no provision is made for visitors with disabilities. But Beijing's broad, smooth streets are far more user-friendly than those of many other cities. Buses are best avoided—they are overcrowded and jerky. Ramps are not provided for wheelchair users at the time of writing, but this may be rectified before the 2008 Olympics.

Living
Beijing

Beijing Now

Above: *Beijing's busy ring-road system, seen from Longtan Park in central Beijing*
Right: *A child sitting in one of the courtyards of the Forbidden City in Beijing*

China's capital is a city preparing to meet and welcome the world. Nearly everything about Beijing is undergoing a transformation in anticipation of the 2008 Olympics, which will be held here. City officials are building new high-rise apartments and business centers, making room for more parks, improving infrastructure, and prepping its people to meet the world.

As China's economy has consistently expanded, Beijing has flourished. Now, in this city once renowned for its crowds of cyclists, bicycle commuters share the roads with cars—the number of private vehicles has doubled, to

NEIGHBORHOODS

• If you work your way outward from the Forbidden City, you're not likely to get lost in Beijing. The *hutongs*, in the old neighborhoods, are being razed to make room for new high-rises, so if you're interested in history, be sure to take a *hutong* tour (▶ 20). And don't miss Sanlitun, the unofficial bar ghetto. Many of the hip night spots and restaurants here may be destroyed in the name of modernity—visit while you can.

CHATTERBOX

• Incomprehensible to the unaccustomed ear, the Chinese language is a series of dialects, with a common set of characters. To allow communication between people from different regions, the dialect of Beijing has emerged as the basis for a common spoken language. Known as Mandarin, *putonghua* to the Chinese, it is learned by non-Beijingers as a second language.

The Changlang (Long Corridor), a covered walkway in the Summer Palace, was built at the end of the 19th century

about 600,000, since 1998, bringing with it rush-hour traffic and previously unheard-of honking. And most drivers are new drivers—beware. Homes and buildings are warmer than they used to be, although that step forward, too, has come at a price: Most days, a thick smog hangs low over the city, especially in winter, when furnaces all over town throw black soot into the air. No longer can you see the ring of forest-covered mountains surrounding the city, as you do in old photographs.

But there's a buzz to Beijing nowadays. There's a feeling that anything is possible. Although the military presence is more in evidence here than in, say, Shanghai, especially around Tian'anmen Square, capitalism is flourishing. As figured by some analysts, the private sector now provides

11

Above: *Red flags flying high above Tian'anmen Square*
Above right: *Pedicab drivers*
Right: *A man relaxes in a doorway of the Laodong Renmin Wenhuagong (Workers' Palace of Culture)*

more than half of all the jobs. Restaurants, bars and shopping centers are thriving. Coffee houses, complete with Western prices, are crowded with locals. The chefs in the swankiest restaurants are world-class.

Less than a decade ago, if you visited the Summer Palace or Tian'anmen Square in winter, most Chinese nationals would have been wearing heavy green army-issued coats, boots and hats. They were cheap and warm. Now, visit the same places and the throngs of locals are wearing knock-off Prada, Hugo Boss and Burberry. Men and women have stylish haircuts, with highlighting and perms the norm, and the occasional blue-haired punk-rock teenager is no longer all that surprising. Women think about the latest fashions; men talk about cars, sports and those women in the latest fashions.

At any time of the year, the elderly—once consigned to the background—are setting up tripods in major tourist destinations and staging family-photo shoots. And they're not point-and-

GOING GREEN

• Beijing is trying to go green, despite a pollution problem. In the works are 800 more green spaces for the city, which should bring the total to 960 by the time of the 2008 Olympics. In 2002, there were a mere 160 parks—but that was four times the number that existed in the 1980s.

shoots, but rather expensive Japanese models, digital and video cameras or multi-lensed professional cameras.

Above: *Soldiers on guard near Tian'anmen Gate*

Don't be surprised if strangers ask you to photograph them with their camera. Beijingers are increasingly practising their English with foreigners. Gone are the days when you would be hard pressed to find English speakers. Now

OUT AND ABOUT
● Beijingers favorite two parks are Jingshan and Beihai, which are where elderly folk practice tai chi (► 54, panel) in the morning. According to tourism statistics 110 million visitors go to Beijing's major parks each year. With new parks on the way, many of which will be free, instead of costing the usual 1 or 2 yuan for entry, city officials expect more local people will use the open space for recreation. Plus, a new law requires ancient parks and gardens to maintain their historic atmosphere. Obeying the law, KFC moved its restaurant out of the imperial-era Beihai Park.

REFORM
● Economic reform is transforming China at an astonishing rate—but at a price. State-run industries that lose money are closed down, resulting in massive unemployment and social unrest. There is uncertainty over the ability of the banking system to handle the country's financial and economic revolution. Political dissent has been crushed for the time being, but can the political order remain immune to change? No one really knows.

13

Modern buildings contrast with the ancient bronze astronomical instruments in the grounds of the Gu Guanxiangtai (Ancient Observatory)

widely available private lessons have given most twenty-somethings, market vendors and taxi drivers on the street an English vocabulary. Scores more speak excellent English. Bargaining for a scarf in the Silk Market no longer calls for hand signals and a calculator. In fact, the number of Chinese studying English is greater than the number of native English speakers worldwide—it is estimated that 1.5 million Beijingers can speak some English, and that number is only expected to rise. Many speak it better than their counterparts in Hong Kong, which was a British colony up until 1997.

MAKING MOVIES

• Beijing resident Zhang Yimou is China's most successful, if somewhat controversial, movie director, with *Red Sorghum*, *Raise the Red Lantern*, *Ju Dou* (the latter two won Oscar nominations) and his greatest hit, *Hero*, to his credit. His earlier films, such as *To Live*, which won the Grand Jury Prize at Cannes in 1994 but has not been featured widely in mainland theaters, have focused on the struggles of China. *Hero*, on the other hand, is a patriotic nod to China's birth as a country in the 3rd century. This star-studded genre martial arts film, in the same mold as the globally successful *Crouching Tiger, Hidden Dragon*, garnered critical success in China, achieved record-breaking sales and premiered in the Great Hall of the People.

Beihai Park, Sazhou Village

You'll also hear plenty of Western music, along with the Mandopop (Mandarin-language pop music) and Cantopop (Cantonese-language pop music from Hong Kong) in the roaring capital nightlife. Beijingers know how to party—and do so as enthusiastically as the residents of any other 'Bright Lights, Big City' metropolis. You name it, you can find it in Beijing.

If you saw Beijing several years ago, you certainly won't recognize it today. Modern Beijing has already arrived.

FACTS & FIGURES

● 1 in 100 Chinese people live in Beijing, which has a population of 12 million.

● A 1995 municipal law decrees that no dog taller than 14in (35cm) can be legally raised in Beijing.

● Beijing's Dongzhimen railroad station can hold up to 14,000 people, more than any other station in the world.

● Some 9 million bicycles are pressed into service each morning.

CITY OF CHANGE

● Beijing is changing rapidly. Be aware that hotels, restaurants, clubs and bars close, move or change name fairly rapidly. English speakers are easy enough to find on the street, but to make travel easier simply ask a staff member at your hotel to telephone and make a reservation for you. Then ask them to write down the name of your destination in Chinese characters to show your taxi driver. Carry the address in Chinese of your hotel to show the taxi driver on the return journey.

Beijing Then

Above: *Ornamental lion overlooking Kunming Lake*
Above right: *Mao Zedong*

'OLD BUDDHA'

Empress Dowager Cixi (1834–1908) first entered the Forbidden City as one of many concubines to a Manchu emperor. When he died in 1861, she became regent to their infant son. From then until her death, she was the effective ruler of China—a deeply conservative figure renowned for, among other things, releasing 10,000 caged birds each year on her birthday and spending lavishly on herself. She acquired the nickname Old Buddha, and following her son's death, chose her nephew as emperor. When he tried to introduce reforms, she had him confined to the palace as a virtual prisoner. The day before she died, she successfully organized his murder.

700BC Mongols, Koreans and local Chinese trade on the site that is now Beijing.

AD1215 Mongol warrior Genghis Khan captures Youzhou (Tranquil City) and his grandson Kublai establishes the renamed Dadu (Great Capital), the site of the future capital, Beijing.

1368 The second Ming emperor becomes the great architect of Beijing, building the Forbidden City.

1644 The Qing dynasty expands the capital over the next century and builds the great Summer Palace.

1860 Anglo-French troops attack Beijing and burn the Summer Palace during the Opium Wars. In 1884, Dowager Empress Cixi commissions a new Summer Palace. Sealed within the Forbidden City, she is oblivious to the poverty in country.

1911 Occupation by successive waves of foreign troops weakens the imperial order. The Nationalist Party establishes the Republic of China.

1928 Chiang Kai Shek controls Beijing until the city falls to Japan in 1937. After 1945, the civil war that began in 1927 resumes between Chiang and Mao Zedong's Communists.

1949 The victorious Mao announces the People's Republic of China, and the remnants of Chiang's Nationalists flee to Taiwan. Soviet experts help rebuild large parts of Beijing.

1966 Mao launches his Cultural Revolution in Beijing, a master move in a power struggle in the Communist Party. Red Guards wave their little red books, and schools close for a decade.

1976 Mao dies, and Deng Xiaoping takes power. Westerners are admitted into China, and foreign investment is allowed in special economic zones.

1989 Students mass in Tian'anmen Square to demand political liberalization. The government calls in the army. Hundreds—possibly thousands—are shot.

1997 Return of Hong Kong to Chinese rule.

2001 China enters the World Trade Organization, and Beijing wins the bid to host the 2008 Olympics.

2004 China's Olympic athletes return from the Athens Games with 63 medals (including 32 golds) and are congratulated by President Hu Jintao in the Great Hall of the People.

Above left: *Detail of the Red Star on the facade of the Museum of the Revolution*
Above: *Tian'anmen Square, one of the largest urban squares in the world*

MAO ZEDONG (1893–1976)

The son of a wealthy farmer in Hunan province, Mao adapted Marxism to suit rural China. When his fellow Communists were threatened by Chiang Kai Shek, he organized the famous year-long, 5,890-mile (9,500km) Long March across 18 mountain ranges and 24 rivers to escape capture. After he proclaimed the People's Republic of China in 1949, his policies dominated Chinese life until 1976. Despite official acknowledgment that Mao made some mistakes, he remains a deeply revered figure among older Chinese, and his influence continues to be felt.

17

Time to Shop

Baked vegetables on sale at a hot stand

From five pairs of socks for a little more than a US dollar to Chinese calligraphy sets, from real antiques to genuine fakes, designer items to knock-offs, you can find it all in Beijing stores,

CLOISONNÉ

Cloisonné is an attractive, colorful enamel finish applied to many types of decorative ware such as lamps, vases, incense burners, tea sets, tables and silver-based items. It is produced by welding flattened wire on to a copper backing to form an outline. Enamel of different colors is then used to fill the outlined spaces with a range of rich shades. An art dating back to the Ming dynasty (1368–1644), it remains popular today.

malls and markets—and don't ignore street-corner hawkers out of hand. Clothes and shoes no longer come in small sizes only. A fattened-up populace—another product of Beijing's rising affluence—means that even normal to larger Westerners can find Chinese clothing that fits off the peg. Larger shoes, tops and trousers are now widely available in both the Silk Market and stores. Moreover, service is increasingly easy to find. Nowadays, shopkeepers will hold up a curtain for you to change behind, or show you to the back room to try clothes on. Many stores have end-of-season sales (March for winter goods and August for summer) that can yield steep mark-downs on high-end fashions.

No matter where you shop in Beijing, knowing your product and buying with caution are key. Check out purportedly genuine Chinese antiques thoroughly, as fakes abound. Even with that caution, the markets—from Hongqiao market, which sells everything from pearls to antiques, to the Silk Market, which sells everything from silk (obviously) to leather boots—are the most fun to visit even if you're not planning to buy anything. Aside from the classic Chairman Mao buttons, curios to look

Below: *A counter in the antiques section of the Hongqiaoshichang market in central Beijing*

Left: *Clothes and textiles stall in Dazhalan district*

CHOPS

Personalized stamps—name chops—have been used for thousands of years in China and, despite mass literacy, are still commonly used. In a number of official situations, where the West would demand a signature, the Chinese stamp a document with their personal chop. The chops are made of a variety of materials—marble, jade, wood and even plastic—and better arts and crafts stores stock a good selection. It is easy to have your name put on one in Chinese characters or in your own language. When making a purchase, be sure to get an ink pad and ink—red is the traditional color.

out for include placemats and napkin sets with chopsticks, hand-painted scrolls, name chops (► panel, left) and mahjong sets.

Some, although not all, vendors can be aggressive, screaming out in English, Spanish, Japanese and Russian to get your attention. But once you're bargaining, humor can rule the day. Beware, of course, the humor is sometimes at your expense: They'll laugh as they try to sell you something that clearly doesn't fit or is clearly not made of 'pure silk.' 'Buyer beware' remains the advice in the markets.

But at other times it is just about enjoying life while working 12- and 14-hour days, seven days a week. In winter, cigarette vendors stick Marlboros in hat-wearing, carrot-nosed, snowmen. In the summer, you may have to interrupt impromtu soccer and hackey-sack games between stall salesmen if you want to get their attention. Go with a sense of adventure, and you're sure to enjoy the day.

Out and About

ALLEY TOURS

Tours of the *hutongs* (ancient city alleys or lanes) start at 8.50am and 1.50pm from the Beijing Hutong Tourist Agency office at the rear entrance of Beihai Park. A 2.5-hour tour of Beijing costs 180 yuan.
✉ 26 Di'anmenxi Dajie, Xicheng District
☎ 6615 9097/6400 2787

Watch towers on a section of the Great Wall (Changcheng), built between the 5th century BC and 16th century AD

INFORMATION

PEKING MAN
Distance 37 miles (60km) southwest of Beijing
Journey Time Around 2 hours by bus
✉ Zhoukoudian, Fangshan District
☎ 6930 1272
🕐 8.30–4.30
🚌 From Haihutun bus station in Beijing (get off at Zhoukoudian)
🚉 From Yongdingmen railroad station in Beijing
🎟 Inexpensive

SIGHTSEEING TOURS

If your time is limited, consider an organized tour, especially to sites outside the city such as the Great Wall and the Ming Tombs (➤ 29, 30). Most hotels have a tour desk, where you can make reservations. Prices vary, so shop around.

The China International Travel Service (CITS) has desks at the Jing Guang New World, Great Wall Sheraton, Kempinski and Hilton hotels. (The CITS main office is ✉ 28 Jianguomenwai Dajie, Chaoyang District ☎ 6515 8565; fax 6515 8192.) CITS offers a busy day-long bus tour to major sights, as well as several tours to the Great Wall, a 7am 'Morning Exercises with Local Chinese' tour and trips to Kangle Palace with its water park, leisure center and bowling alley by day, and to its disco and karaoke club after dark.

EXCURSIONS
PEKING MAN SITE AND MUSEUM

In 1921, excavations near the village of Zhoukoudian revealed evidence of Paleolithic man—*Homo erectus Pekinensis*—dating back over 500,000 years. Bones of more than 40 individuals were identified. You can wander around the site and, in the adjacent museum, see replicas of anthropological finds and remains of extinct creatures that must have terrified Peking Man. The skull of Peking Man disappeared during World War II, when it was taken out of the country for safekeeping and it has never been found.

FRAGRANT HILLS PARK

Popular with Beijingers as well as with tourists, this erstwhile royal hunting territory offers fresh air, bracing walks and superb views of the countryside from the top of the highest peak, reached by cable car or on foot. Mao Zedong

and his revolutionaries lived here before moving to Beijing in 1949. Highlights include the botanical gardens and the Temple of Brilliance (Zhao Miao). Near the north gate entrance, the Azure Clouds Temple (Biyun Si) is worth visiting for the visual brilliance of its stupas, the tiered towers found in Buddhist temple precincts.

MARCO POLO BRIDGE

One reason scholars question whether Marco Polo ever made it to China is that he never mentioned the Great Wall. The Western name of the bridge alludes to his putative 1290 visit and his detailed description of the structure. Spanning the River Yongding, it was built in 1192 and restored in the 17th century, and is noted for an 18th-century stele with a calligraphic inscription by Emperor Qianlong. On each side of the bridge are parapets with hundreds of carved lions surmounting the columns. In 1937 the bridge was the site of the opening shots in the war against Japanese invaders. The memorial Hall of the War of Resistance against Japan (Kangri Zhanzheng Jinianguan), on the Beijing side, is devoted to this event.

INFORMATION

FRAGRANT HILLS PARK (XIANGSHAN GONGYUAN)
Distance 12 miles (20km) west of Beijing
Journey Time About 50 minutes
☎ 6259 1155
🕐 6am–7pm (6.30 in winter) 🚌 333 from the Summer Palace; 360 from the zoo 🎫 Inexpensive; cable car moderate

The courtyard of Shishanlin (Ming Tombs) in Changping district where 13 of China's 16 Ming emperors are buried

INFORMATION

MARCO POLO BRIDGE (LUGOUQIAO)
Distance 10 miles (16km) south of Beijing
Journey Time 45 minutes by bus
✉ Wanping City, Fengtai District ☎ Bridge: 8389 3919; museum: 8389 2355
🕐 6am–9pm; museum 8.30–6
🚌 339
🎫 Inexpensive

Walk

THE SIGHTS

- Lu Xun Museum
  (➤ 57)
- White Dagoba Temple
  (➤ 59)
- Guangjisi Temple
  (➤ 58)

INFORMATION

Distance 1 mile (1.5km)
Time 2 hours including sights
Start/End Point ★
Opposite Bank of China on Fuchengmennei Dajie
🚇 D5
🚌 Fucheng
🍴 Guan Yuan serves outstanding Cantonese cuisine at lunchtime although there are other restaurants in the area

Above: *Fuchengmen Dajie, former home of great Chinese writer Lu Xun (1881–1936), now a museum*
Below: *Interior of the Guangjisi (Temple of Universal Rescue)*

OFF THE TOURIST TRAIL

This walk shows workaday life for ordinary Beijingers and gives you the opportunity to visit several lesser-known places of cultural interest that you might otherwise overlook.

From Fuchengmen subway station, walk the short distance to the junction with Fuchengmennei Dajie, cross the street and turn right onto a side street with food vendors and cobblers on the left. To reach the first stop, the Lu Xun Museum, look for an English sign in blue, pointing the way to a municipal government department, just before a Kentucky Fried Chicken restaurant. The museum is at the end of this side street. Leaving the museum, backtrack to Fuchengmennei Dajie and follow it, looking for a store at No. 165 selling medicines. To get to the Nepalese-style White Dagoba Temple, which towers over this section of the street, turn down the *hutong* (alley) at No. 165.

Back on Fuchengmennei Dajie, you pass a high school that used to be a temple across the street from a large red wall. Head straight across the junction, still on Fuchengmennei Dajie. At No. 25 is the entrance to Guangjisi Temple. At this point, either retrace your steps, or hop on a No. 101, 103 or 42 bus, which take you back to the starting point, where there is a choice of restaurants (➤ side panel).

Bicycle Ride

PARKS AND LAKES

Head south down Wangfujing Dajie and turn left onto Dongchang'an Jie and left again onto Dongdanbei Dajie. The name changes often so ask. You'll bicycle north up this road for 2.5 miles (4km), almost to the Lama Temple (Yonghegong), near the main junction with the Second Ring Road, Andingmendong Dajie (✚ J2). Turn left onto Guozijian Jie, a small street that heads west past the Temple of Confucius. Continue to the T-junction with Andingmennei Dajie. Turn left, and at the traffic lights turn right onto Guloudong Dajie (✚ H3), continuing to a junction by a large red building, the Drum Tower. Turn left here onto Di'Anmenwai Dajie. A few hundred yards (meters) after a McDonald's restaurant, turn right onto a lane, immediately after a bridge.

Follow the lane down to the lake and keep the water on your right as far as Di'Anmenxi Dajie (✚ G4). The rear entrance to Beihai Park is across the street. Turn left onto Di'Anmenxi Dajie, and at the first junction with traffic lights, turn right to rejoin Di'Anmenwai Dajie, the street with the humped bridge. Bicycle south to the T-junction at the edge of Jingshan Park, turn left onto Jingshanhou Jie, and follow the street around the park (there is an entrance on your right) to another T-junction (✚ G5). Go left onto Jingshanqian Jie, and after passing the China National Art Gallery turn right back onto Wangfujing. Enjoy a picnic lunch from a supermarket or street stall in one of the parks.

ON TWO WHEELS

A bicycle tour allows you to experience an essential aspect of Beijing life. You can rent a bicycle at most hotels. Always use the bicycle lanes.

SIGHTS

- Lama Temple (Yonghegong, ➤ 49)
- Temple of Confucius (➤ 48)
- Beihai Park (➤ 31)
- Jingshan Park (➤ 32)
- Forbidden City (➤ 33)
- China National Art Gallery (➤ 56)

INFORMATION

Distance 6 miles (10km)
Time Around 3 hours
Start/End point ★
Wangfujing Dajie
✚ H5 🚍 104, 211

Above: *The rooftops of the Forbidden City and the tall White Dagoba beyond*
Below: *Beihai Park, Sazhou Village*

Beijing by Night

Above: *Colorful and exciting traditional dance*
Right: *Chinese opera in full flow*

AN EVENING OUT

Kick off your night with Peking duck, a Thai curry or Italian pasta in a local restaurant. Dining rooms in the hotels serve delicious food, but, especially for authentic Northern Chinese cuisine, chances are that you can get the same meal for a fraction of the price across the street. And while it's a good idea to polish your chopstick skills before you come to China, be assured that most upscale restaurants can provide a knife and fork if you need them.

BAR HOPPING

Sanlitun Lu is still the hottest street in town. From Durty Nelly's (with chatty waitresses and on-tap Guinness) to Hidden Tree (which serves up tasty pizza and salads washed down with Belgian beers) and the Nashville Bar (featuring live country-and- western music), you can bar hop without ever getting a taxi. Throughout town, any place where you see 'KTV'—for Karaoke TV—is fun to visit for the kitsch factor. But be warned: Waitresses are pushy, drinks are expensive and the bars can be tacky, although they attract a local clinetele, too.

ODE TO OPERA

No trip to Beijing is complete without a night at the opera. Beijing Opera is all-around theater: You get acting, acrobatics, martial arts, dance, costumes, make-up and music. OK, the music is an acquired taste (the word 'screeching' often comes to a first-timer's mind) but it's certainly an experience—simply go for the symbolic painted faces of the opera characters.

NIGHT OUT

If you're looking for the latest club scene, search out one of Henry Lee and Sebastion's venues, the places to see Beijing's young, hip and moneyed —the people for whom a BlackBerry, a mobile phone and at least three designer labels are *de rigueur*. Public Space (➤ 82) is still going strong and they've added Club Look (➤ 80) and The Club (➤ 83) to their offerings— expect techno and house played by Chinese and foreign DJs.

BEIJING's
top 25 sights

The sights are shown on the maps on the inside front cover and inside back cover, numbered **1**–**25** across the city

Summer Palace (Yíheyuan)

DID YOU KNOW?

- The Long Corridor, at 2,277ft (728m), is the longest painted corridor in the world
- Cixi kept her nephew, the emperor in name only, under house arrest for ten years in the Hall of Jade Ripples
- Emperor Qianlong sat on a nearby hill and watched 100,000 workers enlarging Kunming Lake
- The first automobile imported into China, a Mercedes-Benz, is still in the Summer Palace garage

A Summer Palace dragon

INFORMATION

- Off the map, 7.5 miles (12km) northwest of the city center; Locator map A1
- Yiheyuanlu, Haidian District
- 6288 1144
- Daily 7–7
- Coffee shop and restaurant
- Xizhimen
- 301, 303, 332, 333, 346, 384, 904
- Moderate
- Old Summer Palace (► 27)

The largest imperial garden in China, strewn with palaces and architectural flights of fancy, is arguably Beijing's most precious gem. Modern playgrounds of the rich seem dull in comparison with these royal designs.

The ultimate playground Members of Beijing's imperial court selected an area northwest of the city for a summer resort. What you see today was laid out in the 18th century, but toward the end of the following century Empress Dowager Cixi (► 16) misappropriated funds intended for the navy and spent it instead on a lavish rebuilding program for her Summer Palace. Mindful, perhaps, of her debt to the navy, she commissioned the white Marble Boat (a wooden paddleboat structure on a marble base) that is berthed at the edge of the lake. The Summer Palace was ransacked and torched in 1900 at the hands of Anglo-French troops intent on revenge after the Boxer Rebellion, but rebuilding began soon after. A major restoration was completed in the 1950s.

Walking guide Enter the grounds through the East Gate and note first the Hall of Benevolence and Longevity, where Cixi conducted official business. Stretched out behind the hall is the expanse of Kunming Lake, used for skating in winter. Keep it on your left, passing the Hall of Jade Ripples before entering the painted Long Corridor. Near the end of this walkway are a coffee shop, the Marble Boat and a jetty where boat rides and rowboats (or, in winter, skates) are available for trips to the 17-arched bridge, which stretches from the shore to South Lake Island. Plan to spend at least 3 hours here.

Old Summer Palace

The evocative grounds and ruins of the original Summer Palace (865 acres/ 350ha) are enchanting. Stand quietly and you can imagine fabulously clothed emperors and empresses, attended by scores of servants, at play.

East meets West Remnants of baroque pillars and ruins of grand fountains are a tantalizing hint of the artistic exuberance and sheer splendor that once characterized this royal playground. First laid out in the 12th century, it became the emperor's summer retreat from the 15th century until 1860. Artistic styling took flight under Emperor Qianlong in the second half of the 18th century and, though ostensibly created as an act of devotion to his mother, the project took on the feel of an audacious architectural binge. The emperor journeyed south of the Yangtze River, accompanied by artists to make sketches, to fulfill a desire to reproduce in the north the garden landscapes of southern China. The Jesuit architects, Sichelbarth and Benoist, designed Western-style buildings, including gazebos and follies, in a blending of West and East. The results were the Garden of Perfect Brightness, the Garden of Eternal Spring and the Garden of Beautiful Spring.

Elgin masonry The broken masonry of the Old Summer Palace bears testimony to the destructive visit of British and French troops during the Second Opium War. In 1860, Lord Elgin ordered the site to be burned after his soldiers had thoroughly looted it—some of their plunder can be seen in London's British Museum and the Louvre in Paris. Ambitious, commercially motivated plans to restore the entire site are opposed by those who argue the ruins should stand as a historical record of past injustices.

HIGHLIGHTS

- Museum with models and drawings giving some idea of the pre-1860 splendor
- Restored concrete maze

INFORMATION

- ✚ Off the map, just over 1 mile (2km) east of the Summer Palace; Locator map B1
- ✉ Qinghua Xilu 28, Haidian District
- ☎ 6262 8501/6255 1488
- ⏱ Daily 7–7
- Ⓜ Xizhimen
- 🚌 375 minibus from Xizhimen subway station
- ♿ Park: inexpensive; ruins: moderate

Below: A building in the 10,000 Flowers Maze

Great Bell Temple

This unique little museum is in a Buddhist temple where you will see the Yongle Bell, the largest in China. A visit here is a rewarding experience and the music of the temple's Bell Orchestra is a surprising pleasure.

Tons of bells The temple-museum is home to hundreds of bronze bells from all over China, but pride of place rests with a 46.5-ton giant bell cast in the Ming dynasty and known as the Yongle bell. It hangs on a huge wooden frame by a 3ft-long (1m) iron and steel nail coated with copper. The nail is 2 inches (6cm) wide and pierces two U-shaped hooks around the wooden block. It is calculated that each 3/100sq inch (sq m) of the nail can withstand 5.25 pounds (2.4kg) of shearing stress. Displays in the temple-museum (in English) explain the technology of bell-casting in China.

Ring the bells You can get into the spirit of bell-ringing by thumping a large one outside the temple with the help of a small battering ram. Inside the temple, for a nominal fee, you can dip your hand into a large bowl of water before ferociously rubbing its twin handles to produce a musical vibration. If a certain frequency is attained, the vibrations cause spurts of water to appear—thus the bowl's nickname, 'Dragon Fountain.' A narrow staircase leads to a platform above the giant Yongle Bell, giving a history of the bell. The music of the Giant Bell Orchestra may be purchased on CD or cassette. (If you decide to buy one, play it on the temple's music system, before departing, to make sure that your copy works.)

Fine design featuring bells, of course

The Great Wall

Former President Nixon exclaimed to his Secretary of State, 'I think you would have to agree, Mr. Secretary, that this is a great wall.' A visit on a snowy winter day can be so quiet it feels like 'your wall.'

Significance Mao Zedong said that anyone wishing to be a hero must first climb the wall, and for many Chinese people, the wall remains very much a part of their cultural identity. It was built between the 5th century BC and the 16th century AD; its purpose was protective although it served also as a military communications route. From the 17th century onward it was left to crumble away, a process that was speeded by neighboring peasants seeking building material.

Symbol of cruelty At odds with its contemporary significance, the building of the wall was often associated with acts of great cruelty. Emperors like Qin Shi Huang in the 3rd century BC became infamous for their mobilization of enforced labor, and there are stories of sections being made with the blood and bones of their builders.

Avoiding the crowds Ask a few questions before settling for one of the many available tours. Which part of the wall does the tour visit? Badaling, restored in the 1950s, is the most popular location but, be warned, the commercialism and crowds may disillusion you. A cable car helps the large number of visitors. Simatai requires a degree of fitness and fortitude, as sections of the unrestored wall are unprotected at the sides. Mutianyu is accessible and safe and, like Badaling, offers a cable-car ride so it can be overcrowded. Check how much time is spent at the wall; beware of time-consuming and often unrewarding trips to factory stores along the way.

DID YOU KNOW?

- The wall is the only human-made structure discernible from the moon
- The wall's bricks could encircle the earth in a 16ft-high (5-m) wall

INFORMATION

- ✚ Off the map to the northwest of the city; Locator map off D1
- ✉ Badaling in Yanqing County; Mutianyu in Huairou County; Simatai in Miyun County
- ☎ Badaling 6912 2222 Mutianyu 6964 2022; Simatai 6903 1051
- 🕐 Badaling daily 7am–5.30pm; Mutianyu 7.30am–6pm; Simatai 8–5
- 🍴 Restaurants and teashops at Badaling and Mutianyu
- 🚌 Tourist buses 1, 2, 3 from Qianmen terminal for Badaling; minibuses from Dongzhimen bus station for Mutianyu. No convenient bus access to Simatai
- 🚇 Qinglongqiao
- ♿ None 💰 Moderate to expensive
- ↔ Ming Tombs (► 30) usually included in tours to Badaling or Mutianyu
- ❓ Hotels organize tours but consider simply booking a taxi from Beijing for a day

Ming Tombs

Willows whisper in the wind as the stone figures along the Spirit Way stare imperiously at visitors following in the steps of mourners who carried Ming emperors to their resting place.

HIGHLIGHTS

- The mythological *xiechi*, a cat-like creature with horns, one of the six pairs of animals lining the Spirit Way
- The original, unpainted pillars supporting the Palace of Sacrificing, made from entire trunks of the nanmu tree
- Jewelry on show in the Palace of Sacrificing
- The royal treasures from Ding Ling found when the tomb was excavated

INFORMATION

- ✚ Off the map; Locator map off D1
- ✉ Shisanling, Changping County
- ☎ 6976 1334
- 🕐 Daily 8–5.30
- 🍴 Most tours include lunch at the Friendship Store
- 🚌 Tourist buses 1, 2, 3, 4, 5
- ♿ None
- 💰 Moderate–expensive
- ↔ Great Wall (➤ 29) usually included in tours to the Ming Tombs

Below: The main pavilion of the Ming Tombs

Death of an emperor Of the 17 emperors who ruled during the Ming dynasty (1368–1644), 13 were ceremoniously laid to rest in this beautiful place about 30 miles (48km) northwest of their capital. The site was chosen for its geomantic qualities—facing Beijing, with mountains on three sides. Elaborate rites dictated the stages of the funeral. The deceased's concubines were also buried alive to comfort the emperor in the next world.

Not to miss The ceremonial avenue leading to the tombs, the Spirit Way, provides a wonderful opportunity to admire 18th-century Ming sculptures in their original context. Only three of the tombs are open to the public. At the end of the avenue one of them, Chang Ling, comes into view. Emperor Yongle was interred here in 1424, and the focus of interest at this tomb is the imposing Palace of Sacrificing and its collection of imperial riches. A model of the whole site is on show and the exhibits carry descriptions in English. At the rear of the palace, there is a stele tower, a column with inscriptions, while an undistinguished mound behind railings at the back marks the actual burial ground. Of the other two tombs, only the excavated Ding Ling is worth a visit. A staircase leads to the burial vault holding a replica of the excavated coffin. In the courtyard, relics of the emperor and his two empresses are on display.

Beihai Park

Kublai Khan is reputed to have created this popular park, Beijing's largest. Half water and half land, it offers a placid charm and an opportunity to relax in the city, if you avoid weekends.

Imperial landscape The lake in the park was dug during the Jin dynasty (12th–13th century), before the Forbidden City was thought of. All that remains of Kublai Khan's presence is a large, decorated jade vessel that was presented to him in 1265. It is on show in the Round City, inside the south entrance to the park on Wenjin Jie. During the Qing dynasty, Emperor Qianlong (1736–95) directed an ambitious landscaping project that laid the foundations for an exemplary Chinese classical garden. Jiang Qing, widow of Mao Zedong and a 20th-century empress of sorts, visited regularly in the 1980s.

Stroll, row and sightsee Inside the south gate is the Round City comprising a pavilion and courtyard. Beyond, the Hall of Receiving Light was originally a superior gatepost house for emperors and is now home to a Buddha crafted from white jade, a present from Myanmar (now Burma) to Empress Dowager Cixi, who ruled from 1861 to 1908. From the hall, the way leads to a short walk across the lake to Jade Island, noted for the White Dagoba, a 130ft-high (36m) Buddhist shrine constructed in 1651 for a visit to Beijing by the Dalai Lama. Also here is the famous Fangshan restaurant, serving favorite imperial dishes, and a dock where you can rent rowboats. Locals crowd here on the weekends for family picnics and romantic getaways.

HIGHLIGHTS

- The White Dagoba on Jade Island
- Elaborate, imperial-style Fangshan restaurant (➤ 64)
- Dragon Screen, on the north shore of the lake
- 17th-century Five Dragon Pavilions, near Dragon Screen
- Kublai Khan's jade vase, the largest of its kind in China

INFORMATION

- F4/5, G4/5; Locator map D3
- Wenjin Jie, Xicheng District
- 6403 1102
- Park daily 7am–8pm; sights 9–4.45
- Snack and drink shops; Fangshan restaurant
- 13, 101, 103, 107, 109, 111 or 5 from Tiananmen Xi subway
- None Inexpensive
- Jingshan Park (➤ 32)

Detail from the Dragon Screen

Jingshan Park

Get the best panoramic views of the Forbidden City's gold and russet roofscape from the top of the Pavilion of Everlasting Spring. Come here before visiting the Forbidden City and you will understand its vast scale.

Coal Hill As far back as the Yuan dynasty (1279–1368), Jingshan Park was the private recreational preserve for the imperial family. In the 15th century, when the moat for the Forbidden City was under construction, the demands of *feng shui* dovetailed with engineers' need to remove tons of earth. By using this to create large mounds to the north of the imperial palace, the royal residence was sited on high ground and thereby protected from malignant spirits. A story circulated that one emperor kept coal under one of the artificial hills. Coal Hill is another name for Jingshan Park.

Reflection in a quiet corner of Jingshan Park

Vantage point In addition to the compelling sight of the Forbidden City, the central pavilion—perched on the highest point in the park and easily reached from the park's main entrance—also takes in views of the long lake in Beihai Park and its White Dagoba (▶ 31). On a clear day, it is possible to see the Western Mountains to the northwest. The perspective of the city as a whole reveals how remarkably flat most of Beijing is, and it is easy to imagine the force of the biting winter winds scudding across the city.

Dance to the beat Back at the bottom you may catch a glimpse of a troupe of players dancing and cavorting as they lead a re-creation of an imperial procession, with the 'empress' in her sedan, to the sound of court music.

INFORMATION

- ✚ G5; Locator map E3
- ✉ Jingshanqian Xijie, Dongcheng District
- ☎ 6404 4071
- 🕐 Daily 5.30am–10.30pm
- 🚌 101, 103 or Tiananmen Xi then bus
- ♿ None
- 💷 Inexpensive

Forbidden City (Palace Museum)

Wander off the beaten track to imagine the past: emperors and empresses, court intrigues and decrees, palanquins, palaces and thrones. Make no mistake, this was the imperial heart of the Chinese civilization.

A perfect balance No other complex in the world can match the Forbidden City in its harmonious mix of monumental scale, fine detail and geometry. Between 1420 and 1911 it was the residence and court of the Ming and Qing dynasties; today it is a museum complex, formally known as the Palace Museum, including several major sites—official buildings, former residencies, gates and gardens—that are visitor must-sees. Begin a tour at the main entrance, the Meridian Gate (Wumen, ► 53), through the 33ft (10m) wall that surrounds the complex with majestic watchtowers on all corners. The wall itself is surrounded by a moat more than 165ft (50m) across.

Orientation The main buildings in the Forbidden City are laid out on a north–south axis, starting from the south with the Halls of Supreme Harmony (Taihe, ► 38), Middle Harmony (Zhonge, ► 37) and Preserving Harmony (Baohe, ► 36). The Gate of Heavenly Purity (Quianqingmen, ► 52) separates these official buildings from the residential quarter, the focal points of which are the Palace of Heavenly Purity (Quianqing Palace, ► 35) and the Palace of Earthly Tranquillity (► 35). Behind the royal bedrooms lies the Imperial Garden (► 34).

Elitism Ordinary Chinese citizens were barred from entering—they were executed if they did—hence the unofficial epithet. However, it is believed around 100,000 eunuchs served here at the height of the Ming dynasty.

DID YOU KNOW?

- The Forbidden City is the largest palace complex in the world
- There are 9,999 rooms (10,000 would have been hubris)
- Its construction required 100,000 craftsmen and one million laborers
- The Forbidden City was declared a World Heritage Site in 1987
- On average, more than 10,000 people a day come to see the complex

INFORMATION

- ✚ G5/6; Locator map E3
- ✉ Xichang'an Jie, Dongcheng District
- ☎ 6513 2255
- ◷ Forbidden City daily 8.30–5 (summer); 8.30–4.30 (winter). Museum daily 8.30–5; last admission 3.30
- 🍴 Snack shop in the Imperial Garden
- Ⓜ Tiananmen Xi, Tiananmen Dong
- 🚌 1, 4, 10, 22, 203
- ♿ None Ⓜ Moderate
- ↔ Many places of interest in, or close to, the Forbidden City (► 32–38, 52–53)
- ? Taped guided tours in various languages can be rented at the southern entrance and returned at the northern exit

Imperial Garden (Yu Hua Yuan)

A classic traditional Chinese garden, comprising trees and water in harmony with a rock garden and temples. Refreshments here are served in the 'Lodge for the Proper Places and Cultivation of Things.'

HIGHLIGHTS

- Rock garden
- Exhibition halls to the east of the garden
- Top of the north wall and view of Jingshan Park

INFORMATION

- ✚ G5; Locator map E3
- ✉ Forbidden City
- 🕓 Daily 8.30–5. Last admission tickets are sold at 3.30
- 🚇 Tiananmen Xi, Tiananmen Dong
- 🚌 1, 4, 10, 22, 203
- ♿ None
- 🎫 Included in admission fee to Forbidden City

A postmodern display in the highly classical Imperial Garden

Supreme sanctuary There are four gardens within the Forbidden City but this one—some 300ft by 435ft (90m by 30m)—is the largest and most impressive. The arrangement of walkways, jade benches, pavilions and ponds was laid out during the Ming dynasty and, despite the fact that there are 20 buildings dotted around the place, the overall impression is of a relaxing natural setting. The imperial family had the Summer Palace (► 26) and other rural resorts to retreat to *en masse*, but the Imperial Garden (Yu Hua Yuan), at the north end of the Forbidden City, was more readily available.

Repose The artificial rock garden, with a charming little temple perched on the summit, is one of the garden's most picturesque aspects. Large bronze elephants, with their faded gilt, contribute to an air of antiquity that is maintained by the centuries-old cypresses, which look as if they are near the end of their natural lives. Surrounding bamboo plants are readily recognized but there are also other, rarer, plants in some of the flower beds.

Relaxation Most visitors are justifiably weary by the time they reach the northern end of the Forbidden City, so try to allow time to rest in the garden. An old lodge dispenses snacks, clean toilets are available and there are some reasonably interesting tourist stores on the east side (► 74).

Palace of Heavenly Purity

Stories of passion and family intrigue have doubtlessly unfolded in this residential complex containing the private bedrooms of the emperors and empresses: In 1542 a maid nearly strangled Emperor Jiajing here.

Emperors at home Beyond the Gate of Heavenly Purity (▶ 52) lies the more private world of the Forbidden City, where the emperor lived with his family. The Palace of Heavenly Purity (also known as Quianqing Palace), during the Ming dynasty, was reserved as the bedroom of the emperor himself—the empress had her own quarters in the adjacent Palace of Earthly Tranquillity. The Qing dynasty preferred a less formal arrangement. Royalty lived in other rooms to the east and west of the main buildings, but the formal significance of the Palace of Heavenly Purity was not lost. When a Qing emperor died, his body was placed in the palace for a few days to signify he had lived a good life and had died while sleeping in his own bedroom. The successor to the throne was always announced from the Palace of Heavenly Purity.

A red face The palace was the place for the consummation of royal marriages, where the newly married emperor would spend the first days with his wife. The last emperor, Puyi, who came to the room in 1922 on his wedding night as a young teenager, reported as follows: 'The bride sat down on her bed, her head bent down. I looked around me and saw that everything was red: Red bed-curtains, red pillows, a red dress, a red skirt, red flowers and a red face...it all looked like a melted red wax candle. I did not know whether to stand or sit, decided I preferred the Hall of Mental Cultivation, and went back there.'

The imperial boudoir

HIGHLIGHTS

- Hall of Mental Cultivation (west of Palace of Heavenly Purity) (▶ 52)
- Exhibition halls and museums of imperial treasures (east of Palace of Earthly Tranquillity)

INFORMATION

- G5; Locator map E3
- Forbidden City
- Daily 8.30–5. Last admission tickets at 3.30
- Tiananmen Xi, Tiananmen Dong
- 1, 4, 10, 22, 203
- None
- Included in admission fee to Forbidden City (but small extra charge for some exhibition halls)

Hall of Preserving Harmony

HIGHLIGHTS

- Dragon Walk
- Marble Terrace
- Archeological finds from the site, on display inside the hall
- Archery Pavilion (to the east of the hall)

INFORMATION

- G5; Locator map E3
- Forbidden City
- Daily 8.30–5. Last admission tickets are sold at 3.30
- Tiananmen Xi, Tiananmen Dong
- 1, 4, 10, 22, 203
- None
- Included in admission fee to Forbidden City

When you see the remarkable marble Dragon Walk at the rear of this hall, the story of how it got there is a reminder of what the designers and builders of the Forbidden City achieved—all without the aid of machinery.

Banquets and examinations The Hall of Preserving Harmony (Baohe Hall) is one of the Forbidden City's three great halls. Behind it, to the north, the Gate of Heavenly Purity (▶ 52) marks the division between the official, ceremonial sector to the south and the more private residential area to the north. At first, the Hall of Preserving Harmony was reserved for the royal banquets that usually concluded major ceremonial events. Later, during the rule of Emperor Yongzheng (1723–35) in the Qing dynasty, the notoriously difficult higher-level imperial examinations were held here. Successful candidates were assured of promotion to top-rank bureaucratic positions, so competition was intense.

Dragon Walk Directly behind the hall, a broad marble walkway leads down from the terrace and forms the middle of a set of steps. It is known as the Dragon Walk: A design motif depicts nine dragons flying above swirling clouds. Some 10,000 men were needed to excavate the marble; to transport the 250-ton block the 31 miles (50km) from its quarry, wells were dug along the route to provide water, which was poured along the road and formed a carpet of ice, since it was winter at the time. The marble block was pulled along this ice track, it is said, by up to 1,000 horses tied together.

The solid marble Dragon Walk

Hall of Middle Harmony

Best viewed from a distance, perhaps standing on the marble terrace, the Hall of Middle Harmony is a perfect example of imperial architecture. The design demonstrates the popular use of open space to enhance buildings.

Imperial dressing-room Of the three main halls aligned on the north–south axis of the Forbidden City, this is the smallest. It generally functioned as an all-purpose imperial hall. Here, the emperor would be decked out in his fine regalia before proceeding due south to whatever important ceremony or event was taking place in the Hall of Supreme Harmony (▶ 38). Some relatively minor court procedures, such as the formal inspection of seeds before planting, would take place in the Hall of Middle Harmony (also known as Zhonge Hall). This was also where the emperor held audiences with high-ranking court officials or influential foreigners, and where dress rehearsals for various court rituals took place.

A smaller scale The Hall of Middle Harmony is not just a smaller version of the other two halls—it has its own unique features. First constructed in 1420, it was rebuilt in 1627 and the roof design, topped by a ball in its center, is different although it has the same overhanging eaves with decorative figures along the end of each ridge. The smaller size of this hall allows you to take in the harmonies of its proportions, without being overawed by the scale. The interior has a carpeted platform and a large, yellow, cushioned seat that was reserved for the emperor. The interior columns are not as richly embellished as those in the other two halls, but the small squares that make up the ceiling are finely decorated.

DID YOU KNOW?

● The costume and regalia donned by the emperor varied for every event and were all laid down in regulations. Even the everyday gowns varied according to the day of the month—a black-and-white one inlaid with fur for the 19th day of the first lunar month and a sable one for the first day of the 11th month

INFORMATION

➕ G5; Locator map E3
✉ Forbidden City
🕐 Daily 8.30–5. Last admission tickets are sold at 3.30
Ⓠ Tiananmen Xi, Tiananmen Dong
🚌 1, 4, 10, 22, 203
♿ None
💷 Included in admission fee to Forbidden City
↔ Many nearby places of interest (▶ 32–38, 52–53)

Hall of Supreme Harmony

HIGHLIGHTS

- The ornate ceiling
- Richly decorated columns, carved with gold-foil dragons
- The Dragon Throne and the nine-dragon screen behind it

INFORMATION

- G6; Locator map E3
- Forbidden City
- Daily 8.30–5. Last admission tickets are sold at 3.30
- Tiananmen Xi, Tiananmen Dong
- 1, 4, 10, 22, 203
- Included in admission fee to Forbidden City

Here, the court population, numbering thousands, waited in silence as the emperor ascended to his throne, then ritually kowtowed nine times, while the eunuch choir rejoiced in song.

The throne room Inside the Forbidden City, beyond the Meridian Gate (► 53), a courtyard leads to the Gate of Supreme Harmony and a stream crossed by five marble bridges. Two imposing bronze lions stand guard, the male holding an orb in his paw and the female a cub, a symbol of power and longevity. The vast courtyard ahead is dominated by the grandest single building in the Forbidden City, the Hall of Supreme Harmony or Taihe Hall. Here the robed emperor arrived in his yellow sedan chair to preside over important court ceremonies: coronations, royal birthdays, the winter solstice and the New Year. In the marble courtyard stood the armed, personal bodyguards, ceremonially dressed in red satin suits, while members of the royal family filled the marble staircase.

Symbolism The Hall of Supreme Harmony stands majestically upon a three-tiered terrace, with its own small courtyard surrounded by a marble balustrade. The stairway is furnished with bronze incense burners and in the courtyard are further symbols of longevity, bronze tortoises and cranes that have a space inside for burning incense. A pile of grains on the west side of the terrace and a sundial on the east symbolize the power of justice that resided with the imperial government. Entry to the hall is prohibited, but the splendid interior may be viewed from the open doorway.

Smoke wafted from the mouth of turtle-shaped incense -burners

Tian'anmen Gate

Imperial decrees were announced from the top of Tian'anmen Gate with dramatic aplomb—lowered in the beak of a gilded phoenix and received by dignitaries waiting on their knees.

Historic entrance When China was under imperial rule, the gate formed the first entrance to the Forbidden City and served as the ritually ordained point for the emperor's edicts. As such, it seemed an appropriate platform for Chairman Mao Zedong's announcement, on 1 October 1949, to the waiting crowd and to the world at large, that 'the Chinese people have now stood up.' Here, too, in the 1960s, Mao broadcast to the million-strong ranks of Red Guards that the time for a 'cultural revolution' had arrived. A giant portrait of the Chairman Mao hangs above the central portal (portraits of him are now rare in Beijing), with the slogan on its left reading 'Long Live the People's Republic of China,' and on the right 'Long live the unity of the people of the world.' In 1989, student protesters raised a giant statue of a woman holding a torch of democracy, the Goddess of Liberty, to face Mao's portrait.

City bridges The seven bridges spanning the stream in front of the gate were not open to all and sundry—only the emperor could use the central bridge.

Iconography Tian'anmen Gate has become a highly charged icon, not only for Beijing but for China as a nation. Its image is reproduced on everything from banknotes to tourist brochures. However, for the millions of Chinese who want to be photographed in front of it, the experience of being here is important, for its historical significance is deeply felt.

DID YOU KNOW?

- Chinese visitors like to rub the huge door knobs hoping that it will bring good luck
- For a less expensive rostrum view of Tian'anmen Square, use Zhengyangmen (Qianmen Gate ➤ 44)

PLA soldiers on duty at Tian'anmen Gate

INFORMATION

- ✚ G6; Locator map E3
- ✉ Tian'anmen, Dongcheng District
- 🕐 Daily 8–5
- 🚇 Tiananmen Xi, Tiananmen Dong
- 🚍 1, 4, 10, 22, 203
- 🎫 Moderate (free to pass through)

Tian'anmen Square

Kiteflyers and street vendors throng the world's largest square, giving it a festive air, while the monumental architecture is a reminder that the most momentous events in modern Chinese history have taken place here.

Communism's red star atop a clock tower

HIGHLIGHTS

- Chairman Mao Memorial Hall (south, ➤ 43)
- Great Hall of the People (west, ➤ 41)
- Museum of the Chinese Revolution (east, ➤ 45)
- Monument to the People's Heroes (center, ➤ 42)

INFORMATION

- ✚ G7; Locator map E3
- Ⓜ Tiananmen Xi, Tiananmen Dong
- 🚌 1, 4, 10, 22, 203
- ♿ None
- 🎫 Free
- ↔ Many places of interest are in, or close to, Tian'anmen Square

A 20th-century gesture People had gathered outside Tian'anmen Gate since the mid-17th century—it was here that Beijingers assembled in 1949 to hear the declaration of the People's Republic. But because squares are not part of the vocabulary of traditional Chinese town planning, today's vast square, some 2,400ft (800m) long by 1,650ft (500m) wide, was not formally laid out until the 1950s, and it was then almost a political gesture towards a new vision of society. Subsequently, from 1966, vast rallies launched the Cultural Revolution from here, and in 1976 the deaths of Mao and Zhou Enlai (Chinese premier from 1949 until his death) brought millions of mourners to this spot. Then, for two months beginning in April 1989, the square became the focus for the most serious threat to Communist Party rule since its inception. In June 1989, the government sent in troops and tanks to bring student protests to a violent end. Thousands are believed to have died here. The square is now the site for protests.

Atmosphere Little prepares you for the experience of being in Tian'anmen Square. Its dimensions reduce everyone in it to disconcerting insignificance. Most Chinese visitors—tourists from every corner of the country—are as awestruck as foreigners by the colossal space and the cold, gray buildings on either side. The flying of a kite, music tinkling in the background and the taking of photographs add a touch of humanity.

Great Hall of the People

Some troops firing on the students in Tian'anmen Square in 1989 are said to have appeared on the steps of the Great Hall. They may have come via tunnels built for the People's Congress when meeting during a world crisis.

History The Great Hall of the People, which occupies 656,200sq ft (200,000sq m), takes up the west side of Tian'anmen Square. Barring a session of the People's Congress—an event that occurs only infrequently—the hall is open to the public. It was built in the late 1950s, and the monolithic architecture betrays its Stalinist origins. Margaret Thatcher tripped on the steps outside here when visiting in 1982. In 1989, President Gorbachev's entrance to the hall was blocked by ranks of demonstrators.

Sino-Soviet aesthetic The interior design is worth seeing as a definitive example of monumental scale that is seriously lacking in charm. The rooms are cavernous and forbiddingly gray in color and mood. From the Central Hall, stairs lead upward to the assembly hall and the guest hall, fronted by a huge landscape painting brought alive by an ideologically red sun. There are some 30 reception rooms, each named after a region or city (including Taiwan) and decorated in a style appropriate to that area; some are open to public view. The Beijing Room is one of the most interesting, with three different-sized sets of chairs for the different ranks of those sitting on them. There is also an impressive mural of the Great Wall.

Basement shopping The way out of the Great Hall leads down to the basement, where uninspiring stores sell everyday and Western clothes and craft items.

DID YOU KNOW?

- The assembly hall, 246ft (75m) wide and 197ft (60m) long, has just under 10,000 seats and 500 recessed lights in its ceiling
- The banquet hall seats 5,000 guests at a time
- Rooms in the Great Hall are sometimes rented out to foreign companies for conventions

INFORMATION

- ✚ G7; Locator map D3
- ✉ West side of Tian'anmen Square, Dongcheng District
- ☎ 6309 6156
- 🕐 Daily 8.30–3.30 (closed during government meetings)
- 🚇 Tiananmen Xi
- 🚌 1, 17
- ♿ None
- 💵 Moderate

Monument to the People's Heroes

DID YOU KNOW?

- The monument is made up of 17,000 pieces of granite and marble
- 10,000 workers, soldiers and peasants were said to have been consulted over the wording and appearance of the inscriptions

INFORMATION

- ✚ G7; Locator map E3
- ✉ Tian'anmen Square, Dongcheng District
- 🚇 Tiananmen Xi
- 🚌 1, 4, 10, 22, 203
- ♿ None
- 🎫 Free

The monument is charged with past dramas

This monument, the central point in Tian'anmen Square, is dedicated to all those who struggled for the glorious revolution. The site carries a warning to the effect that anyone trying to start another one will be sternly punished.

Heroes of the nation The foundations of the 125ft-high (38m) granite and marble obelisk were laid on the eve of 1 October 1949—the day that the establishment of the People's Republic was announced—but the monument was not officially unveiled to the public until 1958. The inscription on the north-facing side carries words of praise from Mao for all those who died struggling for the country's independence, 'Eternal glory to the nation's heroes.' A similar inscription on the south-facing wall carries the words of Zhou Enlai. The base of the monument is decorated with a series of bas-reliefs depicting key scenes from China's revolutionary history. A graphic scene on the east-facing side shows Chinese people burning the opium that the British introduced into China in the 19th century.

No wreaths, please The two-tier platform upon which the obelisk stands is now closed off to the public and kept under guard—a sign indicates that any laying of wreaths or commemorative gestures is strictly outlawed. In 1976, after the death of the immensely popular Zhou Enlai, anti-government riots broke out when wreaths laid at the monument were removed. Again, in 1989, wreaths laid to commemorate the death of a liberal politician who had been sacked by the government became the catalyst for massive demonstrations that challenged the political order. On 13 May of that year, some 200 students pedalled to the square and launched a hunger strike around the monument.

Chairman Mao Memorial Hall

Millions of ordinary Chinese still have a deep respect for Mao Zedong. A visit to his mausoleum makes this very obvious. Lines of Chinese citizens will wait for hours to file silently past Mao's preserved remains.

Exterior The Memorial Hall, behind the Monument to the People's Heroes at the south end of Tian'anmen Square, was completed in 1977 by volunteer labor, only one year after the death of the famous helmsman of the Chinese people. To date, it has seen more than 110 million visitors. The calligraphy of the inscription above the entrance, 'Chairman Mao Mausoleum,' was the work of Hua Guofeng who briefly succeeded Mao to the leadership of the Communist Party. The two-tiered structure is supported by 44 octagonal granite columns.

Interior Entry to the hallowed ground is through a vast anteroom dominated by a large white statue of Mao. The line of visitors moves forward inexorably into the main memorial hall where the embalmed body lies in a crystal coffin in a gloomy orange light, draped with the red flag of the Chinese Communist Party. You are permitted a couple of minutes to file past the coffin. Photography is strictly forbidden (you'll need to check in your camera, which costs 10 yuan). The mood is somber and reverent.

Technology The body is raised from its freezer each morning and descends after the last of the morning pilgrims. A number of apocryphal stories regarding the problems of maintaining the body gained credence when, in 1998, the mausoleum reopened after a nine-month 'renovation'—looking the same as ever.

DID YOU KNOW?

- Other Chinese leaders have been interred
- The government overruled Mao's wish to be cremated
- 5 gallons (22 liters) of formaldehyde went into Mao's corpse

INFORMATION

- G7; Locator map E3
- South end of Tian'anmen Square, Dongcheng District
- 6513 2277
- Sep–Jun Tue–Sun 8.30–11.30, 2–4; Jul, Aug Tue–Sun 8.30–11.30
- Qianmen
- 1, 4, 10, 22, 203
- Free, but must show passport

An inspiring statue outside the mausoleum

Qianmen Gate (Zhengyangmen)

HIGHLIGHTS

The view from the top of the gate takes in:

- Chairman Mao Memorial Hall (immediately to the south, ➤ 43)
- Tian'anmen Square (to the south, ➤ 40)
- Great Hall of the People (west, ➤ 41)
- Museum of the Chinese Revolution (east, ➤ 45)

INFORMATION

- ✚ G7; Locator map E4
- ✉ Tian'anmen Square, Dongcheng District
- 🕐 Daily 8.30–4
- 🚇 Qianmen
- 🚌 1, 17
- ♿ None
- 💷 Inexpensive

The entrance to the gate is less forbidding than in imperial times

Emperors took their security very seriously—a moat and a large wall ringed the outside of their private city. The remaining portal of Zhengyangmen gives a sense of Tian'anmen Square's monumental scale.

No entry Access to the Forbidden City was simply not an option for the general public under imperial rule; access to the inner city was controlled by a series of nine guarded gates. On the south side of Beijing, Zhengyangmen was the main point of transit between the inner city and the residential areas outside.

City gates The gate was constructed during the rule of Emperor Yongle (ruled 1403–24) in the first half of the 15th century. A sister gate (Jianlou) is clearly visible across the street to the south but, unlike Zhengyangmen, it is not open to the public. Originally, these two gates were joined by walls.

Visiting the gate When you stand with the Chairman Mao Memorial Hall behind you, the ticket booth is on the corner of the left side of the gate, right next to the entrance. Inside, there are three levels. On the first is a gallery of black-and-white photographs relating to Chinese history, with brief explanations in English. The second is filled with fairly uninspiring souvenir stores, and on the third level there is a more interesting store with items devoted to tea-drinking.

Picnics Outdoors are stone tables and Western take-out fast food is available across the street opposite Qianmen subway station.

Museum of the Chinese Revolution

An ambitious redevelopment, due to complete in 2007, will allow the museum to showcase more of its stunning artistic treasures than ever before. There are temporary exhibits until then.

Blowing away the cobwebs The Chinese government has invested an estimated 1.8 billion yuan (US$217.65 million) in the expansion and refurbishment of this new cultural landmark. The shell of the existing building will remain more or less intact, but the imposng 327-yardlong (300m) facade will extend for an additional 76 yards (70m) along the eastern side of Tian'anmen Square. This will double the existing floor space of 101,659sq yards (85,000sq m). The facilities will include a reception area for visitors, a digital cinema, car parking and shops, as well as a research facility and around two-dozen exhibition halls covering Chinese history (including Revolutionary history), art and folk art. During the reconstruction the museum hopes to be able to offer visitors a taster in the form of temporary exhibitions, but there is likely to be considerable disruption.

What to expect The former Museum of Chinese History was founded in 1918, but most of its holdings were acquired after the Communist Revolution. Of the 600,000 artifacts in the museum, drawn from all over the country, visitors can expect to see Neolithic tools, Han dynasty pottery, Ming vases, jade and lacquerware, silk embroidery, ornamental jewelry, stone sculptures and ceremonial armor. There will also be exhibits on modern Chinese history.

HIGHLIGHTS

- The monumental facade facing Tian'anmen Square
- Electronic sign outside which counts down the days, hours, minutes and seconds to the Olympic opening ceremony on 8 August 2008

INFORMATION

- H7; Locator map E3
- East side of Tian'anmen Square, Dongcheng District
- 6512 8901
- Tiananmen Dong
- 1, 4, 17, 57

The new museum is intended to offer a stimulating introduction to modern Chinese history

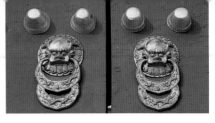

Qinian Hall

The finest temple in Beijing

Through the perfection and harmony of its proportions, this triple-roofed temple, the Hall of Prayer for Good Harvests, achieves a state of both ultra-modernism and sacred serenity. It represents the highest development of religious architecture in China.

Heavenly sacrifices Qinian Hall, or Hall of Prayer for Good Harvests, is part of Tiantan, the Temple of Heaven, the largest group of temple buildings in China. Tiantan Park surrounds the temple off the north–south axis that aligns the major buildings in the Forbidden City. Ming and Qing emperors ceremoniously traveled the short journey south to Tiantan to offer sacrifices to heaven in springtime and at the winter solstice. Before the first Ming emperor made this sacred journey in the 15th century, this area was associated with religious rituals as far back as the Zhou dynasty (11th century BC–256BC).

Floating skyward First built in 1420 and completely restored in 1889 after a lightning strike, the hall was where the emperor prayed for a good harvest. It is an extraordinary structure—three stories and a three-tiered roof, with blue-glazed tiles, rising above marble terraces and seeming to float in the air.

Exquisite detail The four central columns, the Dragon Fountain pillars, represent the four seasons, and the outer rings, of 12 columns each, represent the months of the year and the 12 divisions of the day or 'watches.' The complex artwork of the caisson ceiling, with an wood-sculptured dragon in the center, is best appreciated with binoculars. In the courtyard, south of the hall, one of the buildings has been converted into a large arts and crafts store.

DID YOU KNOW?

- The trees used for the Dragon Fountain pillars were imported from Oregon in the US
- The roof was built without nails or cement
- The number of tiles used exceeds 50,000

INFORMATION

- ✚ H9; Locator map E4
- ✉ Tiantandong Lu, Chongwen District
- ☎ 6702 8866
- 🕐 Daily 8–5
- 🚌 6, 15, 17, 20, 35, 39, 43, 106
- ♿ Cobbled ramp at the west entrance to street level
- 💵 Moderate; park inexpensive
- ❓ Audio tours

Imperial Vault of Heaven

Here, Ming emperors clothed in sacrificial robes, consulted their ancestors' tablets before ceremonially ascending the steps of the three-tiered Circular Mound Altar and reading sacred prayers and performing rituals that had been refined over the centuries.

Interior design is the highlight of the Imperial Vault of Heaven

Wooden temple From the Gate of Prayer for Good Harvests, a raised walkway leads to the Imperial Vault of Heaven. Constructed entirely of wood, it is an octagonal vault with a double-eaved roof. Dating originally from 1530, it was rebuilt in the mid-17th century. In many respects it is a smaller version of the Qinian Hall, with a similar blue-tiled roof, to represent heaven, but it receives more light, so it's easier to appreciate the elegant art inside.

Echoes and more echoes Surrounding the Imperial Vault of Heaven is the Echo Wall, so-called because of its acoustic property, which allows two people standing next to it to converse at a distance. Additionally, in the courtyard, at the foot of the staircase, the first stone is said to generate one echo, the second stone two echoes, while a single clap or shout from the third stone produces three echoes.

Circular Mound Altar (Huanquitan) This huge round altar, south of the Imperial Vault of Heaven, is not as impressive as the other buildings of Tiantan, but its symbolism is highly charged and it is the Altar of Heaven itself. The three marble tiers symbolize earth, man and heaven and, according to Chinese cosmology, the central stone in the top tier marks the very center of the world. On the winter solstice, the emperor ascended to this spot and from a stone tablet read sacred prayers of indulgence.

HIGHLIGHTS

- Bridge of Vermilion Stairs leading to the Imperial Vault of Heaven
- Coffered ceiling of the Imperial Vault of Heaven
- Echo Wall and Echo Stones
- View of the Imperial Vault from the top tier of the Circular Mound Altar

INFORMATION

- ✚ H10; Locator map E4
- ✉ Tiantandong Lu, Chongwen District
- ☎ 6702 8866
- ⏰ Daily 8.30–4.30
- 🚌 6, 15, 17, 20, 35, 39, 43, 106
- ♿ None
- 🎫 Entrance charge included in ticket for Qinian Hall
- ↔ Qinian Hall (► 46), Beijing Natural History Museum (► 56)
- ❓ Audio tours

47

Temple of Confucius

Seek out this temple down an ancient *hutong*. Cooling cypresses in the courtyard lead to the tranquil temple with its commemorative arches over the doorway.

HIGHLIGHTS

- 700-year-old cypress tree
- Hall of Great Achievements
- Steles in the courtyard

INFORMATION

- J2; Locator map E2
- Guozijian Jie, Dongcheng District
- 8401 1977
- Daily 8.30–5
- Yonghegong
- 13, 113, 104, 108
- None
- Inexpensive
- Lama Temple (Yonghegong) (➤ 49)

Examination successes recorded for posterity

Confucius says This noted philosopher and teacher (551–479BC) taught the virtues of moderation, family piety and nobility of mind through good behavior. His conservative belief in the natural hierarchy of the ruler and subject won his ideology the favor of the emperors and, despite fierce criticism from the Communist Party, the influence of Confucius is still felt in Chinese society today.

Outside the temple Occupying the forecourt area are a number of cypress trees including an ancient one that is supposed to have been planted when the temple was built in the 14th century. The other notable feature is a collection of some 190 steles that record the names of candidates who, between 1416 and 1904, successfully passed the notoriously severe civil service examinations. Adjoining the temple stands the Imperial College, now called the Capital Library, where the emperor would deliver his annual lecture on classic Confucian texts. Stone tablets recording the texts are in a nearby courtyard of their own.

Inside The Temple of Confucius, built in 1302 and restored in 1411, does not contain any statues of the philosopher himself, but in the Hall of Great Achievements, the central altar contains a small wooden tablet dedicated to his memory. Emperors and high-ranking scholars came here to make offerings to the spirit of Confucius and conduct ancient rituals. Part of the temple is now the Capital Museum, housing an array of ritual implements used in the temple ceremonies.

Lama Temple (Yonghegong)

This is undoubtedly the liveliest functioning temple in Beijing—colorful and exciting, redolent of incense and as popular with worshipers as with tourists.

From palace to lamasery Built in 1694, this was the residence of Yongzheng, a son of Emperor Kangxi, until 1723, when the son became the new emperor. Following imperial tradition, his former house was converted to a temple and in 1744 it became a lamasery—a monastery for Tibetan and Mongolian Buddhist monks. Closed down during the Cultural Revolution, but saved from destruction by deputy prime minister Zhou Enlai, the Lama Temple reopened in 1980 as a functioning monastery with monks from Mongolia. It has been suggested that the place is purely a showcase exercise in public relations, designed to demonstrate how the Chinese state tolerates Tibetan Buddhism. It has lovely gardens and a wonderful interior.

Layout The temple is a complex of halls and courtyards with a variety of interesting pavilions on either side. In the Hall of Celestial Kings, giant guardians flank a lovely buddha, who is smiling and rotund. The next hall, the Hall of Eternal Harmony, has three buddhas accompanied by 18 disciples. Beyond the next courtyard lie the Hall of Eternal Protection and the Hall of the Wheel of Law (the law being the cycle of death and rebirth). The final hall, the Wanfu Pavilion, contains a 75ft-high (23m) buddha, carved in the mid-18th century from a single sandalwood tree from Tibet, and also flanked by guardians. A wonderful figure of a god with at least 30 hands is the focus of the Esoteric Hall (► 52), on the temple's east side. One of two halls with the same name, it was used as a place of scholarship for the study of scriptures.

Lama Temple's characteristic flamboyant eaves

HIGHLIGHTS

- Maitreya Buddha in the Wanfu Pavilion
- Hall of Eternal Harmony
- Prayer wheel

INFORMATION

- ✚ J2; Locator map E2
- ✉ Yonghegong Dajie, Beixinqia, Dongcheng District
- ☎ 6404 4499
- ◷ Daily 9–4.30
- Ⓨ Yonghegong
- ▤ 13, 62, 116
- 🅸 Inexpensive
- ⬌ Temple of Confucius (► 48)

49

Ancient Observatory

Explore centuries of astronomy in China through the range of star-gazing paraphernalia on display here in a corner tower of the city's walls with fine city views from the roof.

HIGHLIGHTS

- 4,500-year-old pottery jar with pictographic solar patterns
- Star map from Song dynasty (13th century)
- Equatorial armilla of 1673
- Views of the city from the roof of the tower

INFORMATION

- ✚ K7; Locator map F3
- ✉ 2 Dongbiaobei Hutong, Jianguomennei Dajie
- ☎ 6524 2202
- 🕘 Apr–Sep daily 9–6; Oct–Mar 9–11, 1–4
- 🚇 Jianguomen
- 🚌 1, 4, 9, 10, 43, 103, 403
- ♿ None
- 🎫 Inexpensive

These original instruments were installed by Jesuit missionaries

Viewing the skies In the 13th century Kublai Khan founded an observatory near the present site, building on a Chinese tradition that was already well established. Islamic scientists were in charge in the early 17th century and when Jesuit missionaries arrived in Beijing they astonished the court by their ability to make astronomical forecasts and soon found themselves in charge of the observatory. New instruments were installed, and the Jesuits remained until the early 19th century. In 1900, French and German troops stole many of the instruments; they were later returned.

What to see At street level, on the other side of the entrance booth, a small open-air area displays reproductions of astronomical instruments. Also on street level is a small museum with explanations (in English) of the main exhibits. These include a copy of the world's oldest astronomical account, a 14th-century record of a supernova. Steps lead up to the top of the tower, and on the roof there are eight original instruments—including a sextant, a theodolite, a quadrant and an altazimuth—most made in the 17th century. Back at street level, the small rear garden contains more reproductions of celestial instruments as well as stone carvings recording constellations and solar eclipses. An interesting little store there sells small replicas of astronomical instruments, and the Friendship Store is on the same road (▶ 74).

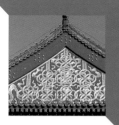

BEIJING's
best

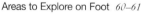

Gates & Halls

In the Top 25

**🟦 HALL OF PRESERVING HARMONY
(BAOHE HALL) (▶ 36)**

CONCUBINES AND EUNUCHS

The majority of the thousands of inhabitants of the inner court of the Forbidden City were either concubines or eunuchs; most were recruited from the poor, and although a few became important and influential figures, the majority were little better than slaves. However, young men volunteered to become eunuchs because it was seen as an honor and at the height of the Ming dynasty there were some 60,000–100,000 court eunuchs.

A symbol of well-being and an assured future in China

ESOTERIC HALL

Of the two halls of this name in the Lama Temple (▶ 49), the more interesting is on the right (east) side as you walk through the temple from the entrance. It was once a place of scholarship for the study of scriptures. The focus of interest today is a wonderful figure of a god with at least 30 hands.

➕ J2 ✉ Yonghegong Dajie, Beixinqiao, Dongcheng District ☎ 6404 4499 🕐 9–4.30 🚇 Yonghegong ✋ Inexpensive

GATE OF HEAVENLY PURITY

This gate divides the official ceremonial buildings of the Forbidden City from the private inner court of residential rooms. During the Qing dynasty, state officials were sometimes granted an audience here with the emperor. Two gilded bronze lions sit before the gate, the female clutching an upturned cub, symbol of prosperity, in her paw while the male grips an orb, symbol of authority, in his claw.

➕ G5 ✉ Xichang'an Jie, Dongcheng District ☎ 6513 2255 🕐 8.30–5 (last tickets 3.30) 🍴 Snack shop in the Imperial Garden 🚇 Tiananmen Xi, Tiananmen Dong ✋ Moderate (included in entrance ticket to Forbidden City)

HALL OF MENTAL CULTIVATION (YANGXINDIANG)

One of the many private rooms on the west side of the northern half of the Forbidden City, this hall was home to Empress Dowager Cixi as also used by the emperor Puyi, as a private bedroom.

➕ G5 ✉ Xichang'an Jie, Dongcheng District ☎ 6513 2255 🕐 8.30–5 (last tickets 3.30) 🍴 Snack shop in the Imperial Garden 🚇 Tiananmen Xi, Tiananmen Dong ✋ Moderate (included in entrance ticket to Forbidden City)

HALL OF UNION

The Hall of Union, standing between the Palace of Heavenly Purity (▶ 35) and the Palace of Earthly Tranquillity, is the middle of the three inner halls in the residential area of the Forbidden City. During the Qing dynasty, it was used for royal birthdays and coronations. It now contains a set of imperial jade seals, a glockenspiel and an 18th-century clepsydra, a time-measuring device worked by flowing water.

🚩 G5 ✉ Xichang'an Jie, Dongcheng District ☎ 6513 2255 🕐 8.30–5 (last tickets 3.30) 🍴 Snack shop in the Imperial Garden 🚇 Tiananmen Xi, Tiananmen Dong ♿ None 💰 Moderate (included in entrance ticket to Forbidden City)

MERIDIAN GATE (WUMEN)

This is the largest and most important of the four entrance gates to the Forbidden City. Usually only the emperor could use the center of the five arched portals, but exceptions were made for the empress on her wedding day and for the three candidates who gained the highest marks in each year's imperial examinations, who used the gate once. From here, the emperor passed sentence on the captured soldiers of defeated armies, inspected his troops and presented the New Year's calendar to court officials. Today's U-shaped, multi-eaved gate dates back to the 17th century when it was substantially restored.

🚩 G6 ✉ Xichang'an Jie, Dongcheng District ☎ 6513 2255 🕐 8.30–5 (last tickets 3.30) 🍴 Snack shop in the Imperial Garden 🚇 Tiananmen Xi, Tiananmen Dong ♿ None 💰 Moderate (included in entrance ticket to Forbidden City)

One of the five towers adding majesty to the Meridian Gate

SHENWU GATE

Shenwumen (Gate of Spiritual Prowess) is the northern gate of the Forbidden City, built in 1420. Each day, at dawn and dusk, the bell was rung 108 times, followed by the drum. Every three years, the girls selected as concubines used Shenwu to enter the palace. The tower, which gives good views across to Jingshan Park, can be reached by a long ramp. It contains an exhibition related to the architecture of the Forbidden City (explanations in Chinese only).

🚩 G5 ✉ Jingshanqian Jie, Dongcheng District ☎ 6513 2255 🕐 8.30–5 (last tickets 3.30) 🍴 Snack shop in the Imperial Garden 🚇 Tiananmen Xi, Tiananmen Dong ♿ None 💰 Moderate (included in entrance ticket to Forbidden City)

FENG SHUI

Literally 'wind and water,' *feng shui* is the ancient Chinese system of geomancy that is used to determine the most propitious design and position for buildings. Today, *feng shui* experts are still often consulted before the plans for a new building are finalized. They employ the same principles as those that governed the layout of the Forbidden City.

Parks

An unusual pictorial display in the heart of Ritan Park

TAI CHI

This form of spiritual exercise, which is rooted in martial arts and sometimes known as 'shadow boxing,' is best appreciated when observed *en masse* in Beijing's public parks from around 6 to 8am. It is particularly popular with older citizens and consists of slow, balletic movements of the limbs designed to balance the flow of energy (*chi*) through the body to attain a healthy spiritual poise.

In the Top 25

DITAN PARK

Conveniently close to a subway station and the colorful Yonghegong (Lama Temple, ► 49), Ditan (Temple of Earth) Park dates to the early 16th century when it was built for emperors to offer sacrifices to heaven. The original altar is now part of a small museum that also displays an imperial sedan.

➕ J1/2 ✉ Andingmenwai Dajie, Dongcheng District ☎ 6421 4657 🕐 6am–9pm 🚇 Yonghegong ♿ None 💶 Inexpensive

GRAND VIEW GARDENS (DAGUANYUAN PARK)

Laid out in the 1980s as part of a project to film the 18th-century classic Chinese novel *The Dream of the Red Mansion*, this is a pleasant place, away from the city center, with a strange artificial rock formation, a water pavilion and walkways around a lake. Readers of the novel may recognize some locations.

➕ C10 ✉ Nancaiyuan Jie, Xuanwu District ☎ 6354 4994 🕐 8.30–4.30 🚌 12, 19, 59 ♿ None 💶 Inexpensive

RITAN PARK

Ritan (Temple of the Sun) Park developed out of a 16th-century altar site where the emperor made sacrificial offerings to the sun god. Situated in the heart of embassy-land, near the Friendship Store (► 74, 76) and the Russian market (► 76–77), it makes for a pleasant evening stroll.

➕ L6 ✉ Ritan Lu, Chaoyang District ☎ 8563 5438 🕐 6.30am–8.30pm 🍴 Restaurant in northeast corner of park 🚌 1, 4, 9, 29, 48, 57, 103 ♿ Few 💶 Inexpensive

TAORANTING PARK
The first park here was laid out in the Liao period (947–1125) and during the Qing dynasty it became one of the few parks open to the public. Its swimming pool is a big draw for Chinese families, but there are quiet places to retreat to, including the remains of a monastery and a number of pavilions (this is also known as Joyous Pavilion Park).

➕ F10 ✉ 19 Taiping Jie, Xuanwu District ☎ 6353 2385 🕐 6am–10pm 🚌 14 from Hepingmen subway or 59 from Qianmen ♿ None 💲 Inexpensive

Youngsters enjoying a snack outdoors

TUANJIEHU PARK
This delightful little park, surrounded by high-rise office blocks and off the tourist trail, offers a relaxing diversion from palaces and stores. Paths lead through a scenic arrangement of lake, willow trees, humped bridge and greenery. There is a small amusement park with rides for toddlers.

➕ N5 ✉ 16Tuanjiehu Nanlu, Chaoyang District ☎ 8597 3603 🕐 6.30am–9pm 🍴 Asian Star restaurant (▶ 68) 🚌 43, 115 ♿ Few 💲 Inexpensive

ZHONGSHAN PARK
This park, southwest of the Forbidden City, opened to the public in 1924 and was later dedicated to Sun Yat Sen, leader of the 1911 revolution and the country's first president. In imperial times, it was the site of an altar, built in 1421 but still standing, where the emperor made twice-yearly sacrifices. Now, ancient cypresses shade locals and tourists alike and there is a children's play area.

➕ G6 ✉ 64 Xichang'an Jie, west of Tian'anmen Square, Dongcheng District ☎ 6605 5431 🕐 6.30am–7pm 🚇 Tiananmen Xi ♿ None 💲 Inexpensive

ZIZHUYUAN PARK
Especially appealing, 'Purple Bamboo Park' is famous for its abundant bamboo (whether there is any hint of purple is debatable). One fourth of the 116 acres (47ha) consists of lakes and rivers; a variety of trees and shrubs ensure delightful arboreal views.

➕ A2/3 ✉ Baishiqiao Lu, Haidian District 🕐 6am–8pm 🍴 Restaurants at New Century Hotel (▶ 86) 🚇 Xizhimen ♿ Few 💲 Free

PARK LIFE

Western-style disco-dancing has become popular with middle-aged citizens as a form of exercise. Early in the morning they arrive with cassette players and the occasional boom box, while alongside them more sedate movements are played out by tai chi devotees. Elderly men stroll with their bird-cages or sit and listen to the warbling of caged finches and orioles. Nearby, affectionate young couples enjoy the relative privacy of parks to neck on benches.

55

Museums and Galleries

LU XUN

Hailed as the most progressive modern Chinese writer, Lu Xun (1881–1936) gave up a career in medicine to become a satirical writer. Both *Diary of a Madman* and *The True Story of Ah Q* have been translated into English and are well worth reading. Copies in translation may be purchased at the Lu Xun Museum.

A bust of Lu Xun

Exhibits at the Natural History Museum

ANCIENT CURRENCY MUSEUM

On the site of the Zhen Wu Museum, a building from the Qing Dynasty, this museum features currency ranging from seashells used in ancient times to the *renminbi* used today. There are more than 2,000 different pieces of currency exhibited ranging from the shells (from the now resort area of Hanan Island) to stone, jade, bone, gold and copper.

➕ F2 ✉ Deshengmen Jianlu, Xiecheng District, North 2nd Ring ☎ 6201 8073 🕙 Tue–Sun 9–4 🚇 Jishuitan 🚫 None 💵 Inexpensive

BEIJING NATURAL HISTORY MUSEUM

This place is unique and very strange. The ground floor, devoted to zoology, is by turns dull and kitschy, but upstairs, under the guise of anthropological study, there are displays of cross sections of human cadavers and pickled organs. Come back another time if a school trip is in evidence.

➕ G9 ✉ 126 Tianqiaonan Lu, Chongwen District ☎ 6702 4431 🕙 8.30–5 (last ticket 4) 🍴 American-style fast-food outlet next door 🚌 2, 25, 53, 59, 120, 803, or Qianmen subway and bus 209 🚫 None 💵 Inexpensive

CHINA NATIONAL ART GALLERY

Situated in one of the first big buildings to appear after 1949, this is the city's major art gallery and China's national art museum. Visiting international exhibitions (details in the *China Daily*) are held on the ground floor. Contemporary Chinese art is displayed upstairs. No Socialist Realism here; the subject matter is Chinese life, especially scenes of rural activity, and

the style is pictorial and mostly Western.

➕ H5 ✉ 1 Wusi Dajie, Dongcheng District ☎ 6401 2252 🕐 Daily 9–4 🚌 103, 104, 109, 111, 112 ♿ None 💷 Inexpensive

FORMER RESIDENCE OF SOONG QING-LING

Soong Qing-Ling, the wife of Sun Yat Sen, the revolutionary leader, lived in this former Qing mansion—home to the father of China's last emperor—from 1963 until her death in 1981. Quite apart from the exhibits relating to her life, the gardens are exquisite and worth a visit.

➕ F2 ✉ 46 Houhaibeiyan, Xicheng District ☎ 6403 5858/6404 4205 🕐 Tue–Sat 9–4.30 🚌 5, 55 ♿ None 💷 Inexpensive

LU XUN MUSEUM

Next to the compound where the writer Lu Xun (► 56, panel) lived for a while, the museum contains drawings with revolutionary themes and material relating to his life, including the furniture from his study and bedroom. No explanations in English.

➕ D4 ✉ 19 Gongmenkou 3 Ertiao, Xicheng District ☎ 6615 6549 🕐 Tue–Sun 9–3.30 🚇 Fuchengmen ♿ None 💷 Inexpensive

MILITARY MUSEUM

Dedicated to the history of the People's Liberation Army (PLA), this museum's graphic displays engage most visitors. The examples of Socialist Realist paintings and early photographs of Mao Zedong are especially interesting. Larger artifacts include a frigate armed with missiles and US tanks captured in the Korean war.

➕ A6 ✉ 9 Fuxing Lu, Haidian District ☎ 6851 4441 🕐 8.30–5 🚇 Junshibowuguan 🚌 1, 4, 57 ♿ None 💷 Inexpensive

PRINCE GONG'S FORMER RESIDENCE

Prince Gong, half-brother of Emperor Xianfeng, occupied this mansion in the mid-19th century, though it dates back to 1777. The main attraction for foreign visitors is the traditional Chinese garden, replete with rockeries and watercourses.

➕ G3 ✉ 17 Qianhai Xijie, Xicheng District ☎ 6616 8149 🕐 Daily 8.30–4.30 🚌 107, 111, 118 ♿ None 💷 Moderate

XU BEIHONG MEMORIAL HALL

Relatively unknown in the West, Xu Beihong (1895–1953) is China's foremost modern artist. The galleries display many of his paintings, including those of galloping horses for which he is most famous. Reproductions are on sale in the museum store.

➕ E2 ✉ 53 Xinjiekoubei Dajie, Xicheng District ☎ 6225 2265 🕐 Tue–Sun 9–noon, 1–5 🚇 Jishuitan ♿ None 💷 Inexpensive

XU BEIHONG

Shanghai artist Xu Beihong (1895–1953) experienced dreadful poverty as a teenager. His father died and he looked after his family. Later he traveled to France and became interested in the avant-garde, but he never lost interest in depicting Chinese life, and his political radicalism ensured his fame.

Xu Beihong is renowned for his paintings of horses

Temples, Churches & Mosques

RELIGION

Taoism, Buddhism and Confucianism are the main belief systems of Chinese religion. The government professes atheism and, while the freedom to practice religion is somewhat tolerated, there is strict control over places of worship (any new place of worship requires government approval). Contact with religious organizations outside China is not allowed. Mosques, Christian churches and Jewish Sabbath services also meet the needs of the city's worshipers. Ask your concierge for details of service hours.

In the Top 25

9 GREAT BELL TEMPLE (➤ 28)
22 IMPERIAL VAULT OF HEAVEN (➤ 47)
23 TEMPLE OF CONFUCIUS (➤ 48)
24 LAMA TEMPLE (YONGHEGONG) (➤ 49)

BAIYUN GUAN TEMPLE

This Taoist temple, whose name means 'White Cloud,' dates back to the Tang dynasty. A factory during the Cultural Revolution, it has been restored and is now busy with Taoist priests and worshipers. The temple decorations include many familiar Taoist symbols such as the Linghzi mushrooms, cranes and storks. A giant ancient coin is one of the highlights.

🞣 C7 ✉ 6 Baiyunguan Jie, Xibianmenwai, Xuanwu District ☎ 6346 3531 🕐 8.30–4 🚇 Fuxingmen 🚻 None 🎟 Inexpensive

BEITANG (NORTHERN CATHEDRAL)

Built toward the end of the 19th century, the church—like many places of worship both Christian and non-Christian—was turned into a factory during the Cultural Revolution. Repair work was completed in the 1980s and Masses are again held (in Latin and Chinese).

🞣 F4/5 ✉ 33 Xishiku Dajie, Xicheng District ☎ 6617 5198 🕐 Services in Chinese Mon–Sat 6–8pm, Sun 6–9.30am and 6–7.30pm 🚌 38, 47 🚻 None 🎟 Free

The Fayuansi Temple

FAYUAN SI TEMPLE

This delightful Buddhist temple, with its six lilac-decked courtyards, is now a college for novice monks, whose earnest, saffron-robed figures can be seen at their studies. The first temple on this site was founded in AD645, and earlier buildings served many purposes, including that of an examination hall. Look for the display of illustrated moralizing texts on the right side as you go through the hallway leading to the main temple building.

🞣 E9 ✉ 7 Fayuansi/Quianjie, Xuanwu District ☎ 6353 3966 🕐 Thu–Tue 8.30–11.30, 1.30–3.30 🚌 61, 109 🚻 None 🎟 Inexpensive

GUANGJISI TEMPLE

A busy, functioning Buddhist temple redolent of incense, visited by a constant stream of devout worshipers. See it as part of a walk (➤ 22).

🞣 E4/5 ✉ 25 Fuchengmennei Dajie, Xicheng District ☎ 6616 0907 🕐 8.30–4.30 🍴 ➤ 22 🚇 Fuchengmen 🚻 None 🎟 Free

NANTANG CATHEDRAL (SOUTHERN CATHEDRAL/ ST. MARY'S CHURCH)

Catholicism came to Beijing in the 17th century when Jesuit scholars were welcomed for their scientific, and specifically astronomical, knowledge. Nantang Cathedral is built on the spot where the most famous of these Jesuits, Matteo Ricci, lived.

➕ E7 ✉ Xuanwumendong Dajie, Xuanwu District ☎ 6602 5221
🕐 Services in Latin Mon–Fri, Sun 6am, Sat 6.30am; service in English Sun 10am ⓜ Xuanwumen ♿ None

The interior of South Cathedral

NIUJIE MOSQUE

The Chinese-style facade resembles that of a temple, but this is the largest mosque in Beijing—and the oldest, founded in the late 10th century. Non-Muslims are allowed into the courtyard, but not the central prayer hall which houses the tombs of Muslim missionaries to China during the Yuan dynasty (1206–1368). The tower was used for observing the moon and calculating the time of Ramadan.

➕ D9 ✉ 88 Niu Jie, Xuanwu District ☎ 6353 2564
🕐 7am–9.20pm 🚌 6 or subway Changchungjie, then bus 61
♿ None 🎫 Inexpensive

WHITE DAGOBA (WHITE PAGODA) TEMPLE

It is not easy to miss this 150ft-high (45m) pagoda, the largest in Beijing, built in the 13th century as a showpiece of the new Mongol capital. It was closed down and used as a factory in the Cultural Revolution. The Nepalese influence in its construction is still apparent. The pagoda is officially known as the Temple of the Miraculous Response.

➕ D4 ✉ Fuchengmennei Dajie, Xicheng District ☎ 6616 0211
🕐 9–4.30 ⓜ Fuchengmen ♿ None 🎫 Inexpensive

WUTA (FIVE-PAGODA) TEMPLE

Established in the 15th century, this little-visited Indian-style temple and its adjoining Museum of Stone Carvings are well worth combining with a trip to the zoo (➤ 62). The temple's pagodas are covered with exquisite Buddhist bas-relief; climb the stairway for a closer view. After looting by Anglo-French troops around the turn of the last century, the temple fell into obscurity.

➕ B2 ✉ 24 Wutasicun, Haidian District ☎ 6217 3836 🕐 8.30–4.30 🍴 Nearby restaurant (Food St ➤ 64) ⓜ Xizhimen 🎫 Inexpensive

ISLAM IN CHINA

There are many mosques in the city and the Niujie Mosque is on the main street of Beijing's Muslim community. Islam was first introduced into China in the Tang dynasty (7th–10th centuries) and is now the religion of various minorities, including the Hui (from western China), some of whom live in Beijing.

White Dagoba in Beihai Park

Areas to Explore on Foot

Sidwalk stalls in Dazhalan Jie

THE FIRST HAMBURGER

The eastern corner of the south end of Wangfujing Dajie, where it meets Dongchang'an Jie (⊞ H7), was the prestigious site of China's first McDonald's. In 1994 the government proposed closing it down for redevelopment purposes. McDonald's resisted, and the media turned it into an international news story. Victory for the government? The fast-food restaurant has now closed down. Victory for McDonald's? There are now more than 30 franchised clones across the city.

BAIWANZHUANGXI LU

This street, south of the zoo (➤ 62), is the Beijing home to the Turkic Uighur (pronounced wee-gar) community, usually resident in northwestern China. Make a late evening visit when the restaurants and street stalls are open.

⊞ A4 🍴 Shish kabobs, spicy mutton and nan bread at most restaurants ♿ None 🚇 Fuchengmen

DAZHALAN JIE

Head south down Qianmen Dajie from Qianmen subway station and keep on the right side. After a string of stalls look for a blue-glassed building on the corner and 'Billy's Shop' across the street. Turn right down the pedestrianized *hutong* (➤ 20). Along the first alley on the left is a centuries-old pickle shop, while back down Dazhalan Jie are musty old department stores with grand architectural facades and an ancient medicine shop. Look on the right for the arched entrance (red lanterns outside) of a famous old fabric store. This is a side of Beijing that is fast disappearing.

⊞ G8 🍴 Fast-food place at Zhengyangmen (Qianmen Gate) 🚇 Qianmen

QIANMEN DAJIE

During imperial times, stores and places of entertainment for common people were not allowed inside the walls of the Forbidden City, so the area south of Zhengyangmen (Qianmen Gate) grew into a beehive of commercial activity, the legacy of which is still evident. It is especially popular with visitors from the provinces, and is an excellent area for foreign visitors to experience a colorful slice of Chinese street life. Qianmen Dajie, the main street running south from Qianmen Gate, bustles with working-class Beijingers. Attractions include a famous vegetarian restaurant, the Gongdelin, at No. 158 (▶ 66); fascinating side streets like Dazhalan Jie (see opposite); and the Natural History Museum (▶ 56).

✚ G8 🍴 Fast-food places and restaurants 🚇 Qianmen

SANLITUN LU

Don't miss this street in the northeast of the city, in an area populated by embassies. It has a character that's not Chinese at all—it's almost Mediterranean. Both sides of the street are filled with bars, nightclubs and alfresco restaurants. It is important to note that black-market traders in the vicinity offer pirated computer and music CDs. Attracts locals, expatriates and tourists.

✚ M3 🍴 Plenty of cafés and restaurants 🚌 115, 118

XIDAN

The main thoroughfare that runs straight across the city from east to west changes its name four times and as Xichang'an Jie runs west from Tian'anmen Square before changing its name again to Fuxingmennei Dajie at Xidan. The Xidan area is worth exploring for its atmosphere, especially in the evenings when lively street stalls mushroom and crowds of Beijingers frantically shop for everyday household items.

✚ E6 ✉ Niu Jie, Xuanwu District 🕐 9am–10pm 🚇 Xidan

WANGFUJING DAJIE

Once named Morrison Street, after a London *Times* correspondent who lived at No. 88, this is one of Beijing's most famous streets. A large part of its eastern side has been extensively redeveloped as a showcase of modern Chinese consumerism (▶ 78), but it is still an interesting walk and a good place to observe Beijing's *nouveau riche* at play.

✚ H5/6 🍴 From fast food to fine dining in hotels 🚇 Wangfujing 🚌 104, 211

CITY VIEWS

The Palace View bar, on the 10th floor of the Grand Hotel (✚ H6), is an excellent place for views of the Forbidden City. The transmission tower for Central China Television also provides a spectacular view of Beijing from 787ft (240m) above the ground (✚ west of A5 ✉ 11 Xisanhuanzhong Lu ☎ 6847 5809 🍴 Restaurant and coffee shop at the top).

Beijing's popular Silk Market attracts locals as well as tourists

For Kids

PLAYGROUNDS

Most public parks have a playground suitable for toddlers and younger children and some of the mechanical contraptions are fun. Zizhuyuan (Purple Bamboo Park, ► 55) is good for rides; boat trips are also available. Older children might enjoy the video arcade in the basement of the Jing Guang Hotel ( N5 ⊠ Jing Guang Center, Hujialou, Chaoyang District).

BEIJING AMUSEMENT PARK

Here, in the southwest of the city, on the west side of Longtan Lake Park, is an impressive range of fun rides—Ferris wheel, roller-coaster, waterslide, boat rides and shooting arcades.

➕ K10 ⊠ 1 Zuoanmen Nei Dajie, Longtan Lake Park, Chongwen District ☎ 6711 1155; www.bap.com.cn 🕓 9–4.30 🚇 Chongwenmen, then bus 8 ♿ None 💲 Expensive

BEIJING AQUARIUM

This attraction, which opened in 1999, is adjacent to Beijing Zoo and features regional marine life. The shark tank and killer whale show are must-sees.

➕ B3 ⊠ 137 Xizhimenwai, Xicheng District ☎ 6217 6655; www.bj-sea.com 🕓 9–5.30 🚇 Xizhimen ♿ None 💲 Expensive

BEIJING ZOO

Depressing by the standards of the great Western zoos, this is worthwhile for its famous giant panda house. Spare a moment for the lesser panda from Sichuan province. Tucked away northwest of the city, the zoo is easily reached by subway but avoid weekends. Visit the nearby Museum of Stone Carvings and Beijing Aquarium to make the trip worthwhile.

➕ B3 ⊠ 137 Xizhimenwai Dajie, Xicheng District ☎ 6831 4411 🕓 7.30–6 summer; 8–5 winter 🍴 Nearby restaurant (Food St ► 64) 🚇 Xizhimen ♿ None 💲 Inexpensive

Youngsters enjoy rides at Beijing Amusement Park

EXPLORASCIENCE

Sponsored by Sony, this interactive science exhibition makes use of the latest digital wizardry as it explores the world of sight and sounds. There are gadgets and activities galore, all designed to amuse the kids while encouraging them to think at the same time. Don't miss the robotic dog!

➕ J6 ⊠ First floor, Oriental Plaza, 1 Dongchangan Jie, Dongcheng District ☎ 8518 2255 🕓 Mon–Fri 9.30–5.30, Sat–Sun 10–7, closed second Mon and Tue of each month 🍴 Cafés and restaurants in the mall 🚇 Wangfujing ♿ Good 💲 Moderate

LE COOL ICE SKATING CHINA WORLD

Dance or race your way around the 957sq yard (800sq m) ice rink where music makes you want to take flight. Some hopeful would-be Olympians practicing with their coaches really do take off.

➕ N7 ⊠ 1 Jianguomenwai Dajie, Chaoyang District ☎ 6505 5776 🕓 10–10 🍴 Food center next door 🚇 Guomao 🚌 1, 4, 37, 52 ♿ None 💲 Moderate

BEIJING
where to...

Northern Chinese Cuisine

PRICES

Average prices, for a meal for two excluding drinks:

Y   under 100 yuan
YY   between 100 and 250 yuan
YYY over 250 yuan

NORTHERN CUISINE

This category of Chinese food–taking in the whole area north of the Yangtze–includes imperial cuisine (reserved, and specially prepared, for the court), Beijing duck and traditional city fare, along with food from remote northern areas like Mongolia and Dongebi. Instead of rice, noodles and steamed bread provide the basic sustenance, accompanied by vegetables and cold appetizers. From the far north come hearty beef and lamb dishes. Street cuisine is quickly cooked food from mobile stalls with hotplates–pancakes filled with cooked vegetables are particularly delicious but it is wise to avoid meat fillings.

BEIJING EXPRESS (Y)

An inexpensive place to enjoy northern Chinese street cuisine in clean and comfortable surroundings. The menu is divided into sections offering noodles, snacks, hot dishes and cold dishes—why not try something from each category? The noodle soup with double boiled spare ribs is worth trying, as are the sautéed wild vegetables with shredded pork.
➕ A3 ✉ New Century Hotel, Shoudu Tiyuguannan, Haidian District ☎ 6849 1114
⏰ Lunch and dinner
🚇 Xizhimen

BIANYIFANG ROAST DUCK RESTAURANT (YY)

This famous roast duck restaurant has two dining areas, one pricier but also more pleasant, with more comfortable seats.
➕ J7 ✉ 2c Chongmenwai Dajie, Chongwen District ☎ 6712 0505 ⏰ Lunch and dinner 🚇 Chongwenmen

FANGSHAN (YYY)

Court recipes once reserved for emperors' 19th-century meals form the basis of the elaborate imperial cuisine served at this renowned restaurant in Beihai Park. Sumptuous imperial-style surroundings.
➕ G5 ✉ 1 Wenjinjie (inside the east gate of Beihai Park) ☎ 6401 1879/1889 ⏰ Daily 11am–1.30pm, 5–8 🚌 13, 101, 103, 107, 109, 111

FOOD ST (Y–YY)

Situated behind the Xiyuan Hotel, close to the zoo, this is an excellent place to try northern Chinese cuisine at affordable prices. There are varied fresh fish dishes, noodles with shredded chicken, sweet dumplings and delicacies such as deep-fried scorpions. The barbecued meat cooked over charcoal and served on skewers is recommended.
➕ A3 ✉ 1 Sanlihe Lu, Haidin District ☎ 6701 1379
⏰ Lunch and dinner
🚇 Xizhimen

KING ROAST DUCK (YY)

If you're aiming to eat Peking duck every night while you are in Beijing, go here. Not only can you get the Imperial duck, but also sides of duck liver and lettuce-wrapped minced duck.
➕ L7 ✉ 24 Jianguomenwai Dajie, Chaoyang District ☎ 6515 6908 ⏰ 10am–9pm 🚌 1, 4, 37, 52

LI JIA CAI IMPERIAL RESTAURANT (YYY)

The founder of this tiny and highly-regarded restaurant was the great grand-daughter of an employee in the Qing court, who obtained the menus for Empress Dowager Cixi's meals. The restaurant, part of a family home, serves imperial dishes accompanied by a small number of Beijing and Li family dishes.
➕ F3 ✉ 11 Yangfang Hutong, Deshengmennei Dajie, Xicheng District ☎ 6618 0107
⏰ Daily 4–10pm (reservations up to 2 weeks in advance are necessary) 🚇 Jishuitan

QUAN JUDE KAOYADIAN (YY–YYY)

The name means 'old duck,' but don't be put off—this is a fine place for a Beijing duck banquet (▶ panel). The restaurant has been in the same family for 150 years and is now the flagship for a group of restaurants including a take-out place next door. Be warned, service is leisurely to slow.

✚ G8 ✉ 32 Qianmen Dajie, Chongwen District ☎ 6511 2418 ⏰ Daily 11–1.30, 4.30–8 Ⓜ Qianmen

RED CAPITAL (YYY)

Reserve a table here as soon as you arrive in Beijing. It's *the* place to go to impress guests. Featuring a 1950s-style cigar and cocktail lounge and a lush courtyard setting, it's genuinely relaxing despite its Cultural Revolution nostalgia. Plus, the Beijing-style cooking is delightful and plentiful.

✚ G8 ✉ 32 Qianmen Dajie, Chongwen District ☎ 6511 2418 ⏰ Lunch and dinner Ⓜ Qianmen

SI HE XUAN (YY)

Black-and-white photographs of old Beijing adorn the walls, in the spirit of the traditional cuisine of the city, at which this restaurant excels. Lunchtime is the best value, with cold appetizers like celery with tofu and hot dumplings, stuffed buns and noodles or *congee* (soupy rice); Chinese tea and pastries filled with lotus root complete a good meal.

✚ M7 ✉ Jinglun Hotel, 3 Jianguomenwai Dajie, Chaoyang District ☎ 6500 2266 ⏰ Lunch and dinner 🚌 1, 4, 37, 52

TUAN JIE HU BEIJING ROAST DUCK (YY)

One of the most economical and visitor-friendly restaurants offering a good Peking duck. There are also lots of seafood dishes, as well as choices that are less familiar to Western palates—like sautéed turtle.

✚ N5 ✉ Bldg. 3 Tuanjiehu Lu, Chaoyang District ☎ 6582 4003 ⏰ Lunch and dinner 🚌 302, 402, 405, 801

XIAOWANG FU'S HOME RESTAURANT (YY)

Famous for Beijing duck, this restaurant also offers excellent sweet-and-sour chicken, garlic-soaked greens and basic home cooking. Outdoor seating.

✚ M3 ✉ 2 Guanghualu Dongli, Chaoyang District ☎ 6591 3255 ⏰ Daily 11–11 🚌 115, 118

YUEMING LOU (Y)

A former church gets a tasteful makeover and becomes a temple to *lao beijing cai* (traditional Beijing cooking) with its uncompromising use of seasonings and rich sauces. Signature dishes include popular standards like *congbao yangrou* (lamb fried with scallions/ spring onions) and *su hezi* (vegetable dumplings).

✚ G3 ✉ 21A Ya'er Hutong, Xicheng District ☎ 6400 2069 ⏰ Daily 10am–11pm Ⓜ Gulou Dajie

BEIJING DUCK... AND MORE DUCK

Slices of roast duck are placed inside a thin pancake along with onion or cucumber and sometimes sweetened with plum sauce or a wheat jam. The result is very rich and it's best not to think about the cholesterol count. A real feast begins with cold duck and ends with duck soup. A side plate of mashed garlic acts as an antidote to the rich, oily duck skin and meat.

ALCOHOL

Beer is available in most establishments in Beijing, but wine and spirits are likely to be found only in places patronized by tourists.

Southern & Western Chinese Cuisine

SOUTHERN CUISINE

'Everything with legs except a table, everything in the air except an airplane and everything under the sea except a submarine.' This Cantonese joke gives a fair idea of the variety of ingredients that go into southern cuisine. Fish–typically placed in a wok and lightly fried or, more usually, steamed, is a special favorite, as are the sweet and savory small plates that go by the name of *dim sum*, eaten for breakfast or lunch.

SICHUAN

Outside China, Cantonese food may be the most widely known regional cuisine, but the western province of Sichuan provides the most surprises to the taste buds. The cunning use of spices, especially red chili, gives Sichuan food a reputation for being very hot, but it is also very subtle. A typical appetizer might be fine slices of beef infused with the tangy peel of a kumquat.

AFUNTI (YY)

Roasted lamb or chicken with nan bread are favorites at this conveniently located Muslim Uighur restaurant. Ethnic music and dancing in the evening make for an enjoyable night out. ✚ K5 ✉ 2a Houguaibang Hutong, Chaoyangmennei Dajie, Chaoyang District ☎ 6525 2288 🕐 11am until the last customers leave 🚌 101, 110, 202

BEIJING AH YAT ABALONE RESTAURANT (YYY)

Run by a chef who views Cantonese food as the pinnacle of Chinese cuisine, this restaurant rivals the best in Hong Kong. If you're really adventurous (and haven't tasted it in Hong Kong, where it is popular) try the edible bird's nest. ✚ L6 ✉ 1A Jianguyonmenwai Dajie, Chaoyang District ☎ 6508 9613 🕐 10.30–10.30 🚇 Guamao

BEIJING GREEN TIANSHI VEGETARIAN RESTAURANT (Y–YY)

Excellent and attractive vegetarian restaurant with mock-meat dishes like deep fried 'chicken', rice with 'seafood' and braised 'eel'. Pictures of famous vegetarians—Shakespeare?—line the stairs. Superb non-alcoholic cocktails, beer and champagne. Snacks and soft drinks are served downstairs. ✚ J5 ✉ 57 Dengshikouxi Jie, Dongcheng District ☎ 6524 2349/2476 🕐 10.30–10 🚌 108, 111

BE THERE OR BE SQUARE CAFE (Y)

Genuine Cantonese food is guaranteed here as the chefs all hail from Hong Kong. The ideal place, therefore, to sample *gulao rou* (deep-fried sweet-and-sour pork with pineapple) and other classic dishes. Don't be put off by the drab location—it's much nicer inside than out. ✚ H7 ✉ BB71, Oriental Plaza East, I Dongchang'an Jie, Dongcheng District ☎ 8518 6518 🕐 24 hours 🚇 Wangfujing

CHAO YANG XIN JING (YY)

Cantonese restaurant serving a range of seafood and, though well off the tourist track, it has an English-language menu. In summer the outdoor tables are crowded until the wee hours. ✚ Off the map, east of N6 ✉ 11 Hongmiao Lu, Chaoyang District ☎ 6502 3327 🕐 6am–3am 🚌 101, 112

DING TAI ZHEN (Y)

The large menu in English includes many fish dishes and old Western favorites such as chicken rice with ginger, as well as unusual appetizers like lotus root. This licensed restaurant is suitable for vegetarians. Try the Iron Fairy tea. Avoid the toilets! ✚ J5 ✉ 116 Dongsinan Dajie, Chaoyang District ☎ 6522 7286 🕐 11–2.30, 6–11 🚌 110, 116, 120, 204

GONGDELIN (YY)

This is a branch of a famous Shanghai

vegetarian restaurant, with its own delightful English-language menu featuring, for example, 'chicken cutlets in the shape of lantern' and 'the Fire is singeing the Snow-Capped Mountains.' The food is excellent and the mock-meat dishes satisfy even the most steadfast meat-eaters.

✚ G9 ✉ 158 Qianmen Dajie, Chongwen District ☎ 6511 2542 ⊙ 10.30–8.30 ⊝ Qianmen

MAKYE AME (Y)

Authentic Tibetan restaurants are thin on the ground in Beijing, but this intimate little diner is the real McCoy, with yak meat among the traditional dishes on offer. Cushions and couches contribute to the restful atmosphere.

✚ L6 ✉ A11 (2nd floor), Xiushui Nanjie, Jianguomenwai, Chaoyang District ☎ 6506 9616 ⊙ 10.30–10.30 ⊝ Jianguomen

THE MIDDLE 8TH RESTAURANT (YY)

Sample the subtle delights of Yunnanese cooking, its scents and aromas reminiscent of Thai cuisine, before hot-footing it to the bright lights of Sanlitun for a nightcap. The name of this chic restaurant, incidentally, refers to its location (Middle 8th Street).

✚ M3 ✉ Sanlitun Zhongba Lu, Chaoyang District ☎ 6413 0629 ⊙ Daily 11–2, 5–10.30 ⊟ 113, 117

NENG REN JU (YY)

If you're looking for Sichuan hot pot with a twist, check out the boiled lamb dish, which is cooked in a soup of vegetables and spices and then served on a separate plate so you can dip the lamb in a peanut sauce with a kick—it's flavored with chili and cilantro.

✚ D5 ✉ 5 Taipingqiao, Baitasi, Xicheng District ☎ 6601 2560 ⊙ 10am–2am ⊝ Fuchengmen ⊟ 7, 38

SICHUAN RESTAURANT (YY)

Overlooks the lobby of the Xiyuan Hotel. Be sure to try the Eight Treasures tea (▶ panel) or the hotel's own strong brew of Kaiser beer. Spiced chicken is a fine cold appetizer and braised fish in black-bean sauce a typical main course. The fried walnuts make a delicious dessert.

✚ B3 ✉ Xiyuan Hotel, 1 Sanlihe Lu, Haidian District ☎ 6831 3388 ⊙ Lunch and dinner 11–2, 6.30–10.30 ⊝ Xizhimen

SUI YUAN (YYY)

Superb Cantonese cuisine in the Beijing Hilton. Specialties change, but you can rely on the stir-fried fish dishes, and in winter the Mongolian-style chicken and beef satay is unbeatable. A Beijing duck set menu is available, and at lunchtime the shrimp dumplings and spring rolls are tempting. Live classical music at night.

✚ N2 ✉ 2/F, Hilton Hotel, 1 Dongfang Lu, Dongsanhuanbei Lu, Chaoyang District ☎ 6466 2288, ext 7416 ⊙ 11.30–2, 5.30–10 ⊟ 302, 402, 801

EIGHT TREASURES TEA

A specialty of Sichuan restaurants is Eight Treasures tea, served from the longest teapot you are ever likely to see. The eight ingredients are: jasmine, jujule, walnut, fruit of Chinese wolfberry, raisin, crystal sherry, ginseng and dried longan pulp. The taste is slightly spicy, and prepares you for the spicy flavors to come.

Other Asian Restaurants

ASIAN FOOD

Not so many years ago, the possibility of enjoying an authentic Indian or Thai meal in Beijing would have been unthinkable. Today, chefs are regularly brought in from other parts of Asia and pineapple fried rice, spicy Thai soup, nan bread, Masala tea and tandoori chicken offer exciting alternatives to Chinese food.

ASIAN STAR (YY)

Eclectic menu featuring Thai, Malaysian and Indonesian fare as well as a host of Indian dishes. Options such as curries and tandoori chicken vie with the Malaysian dishes as some of the best Asian eating you will find in Beijing.

✚ N4 ✉ 26 Dongsanhuanbei Lu, Chaoyang District ☎ 6582 5306 ⏰ 11–2.30, 5–10.30 🚌 113, 402, 405

BOROM PIMAN (YYY)

The consensus among Beijing's expatriate community is that this restaurant in the Holiday Inn out on the road to the airport offers the best Thai food in the city. The service is exemplary and the decor Thai.

✚ Off the map near the airport ✉ Holiday Inn Lido, Jichang Lu, Jiangtai Lu, Chaoyang District ☎ 6437 6688 ext. 2899 ⏰ 11.30–2, 6.30–11 🚌 401, 403

CHUN XIA QIU DONG (YY)

Korean restaurants are thick on the gound in China but few are distinguished. An exception is Chun Xia Qiu Dong, where you should look out for the national dish *Bi Ban Bap*, a rich stew comprising meat, rice and egg, cooked and served in a stone pot. If you're not familiar with the cuisine, opt for one of the attractively priced set meals.

✚ Off map ✉ Chaoyang Park West Gate, Chaoyang District ☎ 6593 6599 ⏰ Daily 11–2, 5–10 🚌 115, 118

HATSUNE (YYY)

Perhaps the best recommendation for this award-winning Japanese restaurant is that it numbers visiting Tokyo businesspeople among its regular diners. The chef uses only the freshest ingredients in preparing the sushi, sashimi and tempura, all of which are immaculately presented by attentive waitstaff.

✚ N6 ✉ 2/F Heqiao Bulding C, 8A Guanghua Lu (four blocks east of Kerry Center), Chaoyang District ☎ 6581 3939 ⏰ 11.30–2, 5.30–10 🚇 Guo Mao

HEPINGMEN KOREAN BBQ (Y–YY)

Korean restaurants in Beijing tend not to translate their menus, so non-Korean diners must rely on photographs or look around to see what is being served. The specialty is barbecued meats: A small grill is brought to the table for diners to do their own barbecuing. Good fun for newcomers to Korean cuisine as well as for old hands—but not for those who dislike hot, spicy food.

✚ G8 ✉ 1–2F West Wing of Zifeng Dasha, 1 Dayabao Hutong, Chaoyang District ☎ 6521 1167 ⏰ 11–11 🚇 Hepingmen

LAU PA SAK/XANADU (YY)

Malaysian, Indonesian and Chinese dishes all appear on the menu of this classy Singaporean restaurant where the quality of the food is consistently good and the prices by no

means unreasonable.
You'll find it just across
the road from the
Canadian embassy.

➕ M3 ✉ Xindonglu,
Chaoyang District ☎ 6417
0952 ⏰ 11–11
🚌 110, 120, 208

NAM NAM (YY

Inside this Vietnamese
restaurant in Sanlitun, the
entertainment area, are
the elegant surroundings
of a French Colonial villa.
A wonderful ambience
and food to match—
altogether an
unforgettable dining
experience.

➕ M3 ✉ 7 Sanlitun Lu,
Chaoyang District ☎ 6468
6053 ⏰ 10.30–10.30
🚌 113, 115, 117, 118

PINK LOFT (YYY)

The chef serves chili-
spiced noodles and fresh
fish from a wooden boat—
a bit like a stage. For
added drama, swish your
Thai favorites back with
Dom Perignon.

➕ M3 ✉ Sanlitun Nanji;
Chaoyang District ☎ 6506
8811 ⏰ 11–11 🚇 Guomao
🚌 115, 118

RED BASIL (YY–YYY)

An excellent Thai
restaurant. The superb
food prepared by Thai
chefs warrants the trip to
the Third Ring Road just
south of Sanyan Bridge.
The menu does not
indicate how spicy the
various dishes are but the
staff are helpful.

➕ N1 ✉ Building 8, Bei
Sanyuan Donggiao, opposite
Jingxin Plaza ☎ 6460 2339
⏰ 11.30–2, 5.30–9.30
🚌 302

SANSI LANG (YY)

The most affordable
Japanese restaurant in the
city. The tempura and
sushi are definitely worth
trying. There are pictures
of all the dishes to help
you choose.

➕ N2 ✉ 2 Guanghua Lu,
Chaoyang District ☎ 6507
4003 ⏰ 10am–11pm
🚌 9, 300, 402, 801

SERVE THE PEOPLE (Y–YY)

It's trendy, near the bars
of Sanlitun and serves
reasonably priced Thai
food. The Pad Thai is
authentic.

➕ M3 ✉ 1 Xiwujie Sanlitun,
Chaoyang District ☎ 8454
4580 ⏰ 10.30–10.30 🚌 115,
118

THE TAJ PAVILION (YY–YYY)

Excellent Indian food for
vegetarians and meat-
eaters. Service is friendly
and the spinach or potato
paneer are rich. Try their
lassi drinks as well.

➕ N7 ✉ 1/F West Wing,
China World Trade Centre,
Chaoyang District ☎ 6505
2288, ext. 80116
⏰ 11.30–2.30, 6–10.30
🚇 Guomao 🚌 1, 4, 37, 52

THE TANDOOR (YYY)

This restaurant has an
established reputation for
top-notch North Indian
cooking. The five-course
lunch menu is excellent
value. Extensive wine list
and live dance shows.

➕ L4 ✉ 1/F Great Dragon
Hotel, 2 Gongrentiyuchangbei Lu,
Chaoyang District ☎ 6597
2211/2299, ext 2112
⏰ 11.30–2, 5.30–10.30
🚌 113, 208

QUENCHING THIRST

Most restaurants serves a
variety of Chinese and
international beers in addition
to other alcoholic drinks, but
for many diners a bottle of
cold mineral water, readily
available in all Beijing
restaurants, is a better
complement to hot and spicy
food. Best of all is a
platter of fresh fruit, a *lassi*
drink (made with yoghurt)
from India, or a glass of Thai
iced coffee.

Western Restaurants

DINING WITH A VIEW

On the 26th floor of the Xíyuan Hotel, the Carousel revolving restaurant serves Beijing and other Asian dishes while taking in panoramic views of the city. The TV Tower (► 61, panel) has a restaurant and café, but its view cannot match that of the Belle Vue restaurant on the 29th floor at the Kunlon Hotel (✚ N2 opposite the Lufthansa Center, ► 78), which takes about 90 minutes to complete one revolution.

ATHENA/YADIANNA (YY)

The only Greek restaurant in the city serves *dolmades* (stuffed vine leaves) and other typical national dishes in suitably Mediterranean-style surroundings—dine out on the patio in summer. Discount for group reservations.
✚ M3 ✉ 1 Xiwu Jie (Sanlitun), Chaoyang District ☎ 6464 6036 ◉ 11–11 🚌 117

BLEU MARINE (YY–YYY)

This oh-so-French bistro with outdoor café-style seating serves up French countryside fare. The sandwiches are hearty and the wine list is reasonably extensive.
✚ L6 ✉ 5 Guanghua Xilu, Jianguomenwai embassy area, Chaoyang District ☎ 6500 6704 ◉ 11.30–11.30 🚇 Yong An Li

LE CAFÉ IGOSSO (YY)

Currently one of the most popular Italian restaurants in the capital, Igosso's hallmarks are its relaxed, friendly atmosphere (children welcome), excellent risottos, delicious homemade bread and eminently affordable prices.
✚ M8 ✉ Dongsanhuannan Lu (0.5 mile/800m south of Guamao Bridge on east side of street), Chaoyang District ☎ 8771 7013 ◉ 11.30am–1am 🚇 Guomao, then buses 28, 52

DANIELI'S (YYY)

You will find Beijing's only homemade pasta served here and a marvelous range of sauces from tomato to carbonara. The salad is fresh and the wines are reasonably priced. It is also great to relax in the big, comfy chairs after a day's hard touring.
✚ L7 ✉ 2nd floor, St. Regis Hotel, 21 Jianguomen Wai Dajie, Jianguomenwai embassy area, Chaoyang District ☎ 6460 6688 ext. 2440 ◉ 11.30–2, 6–10 🚇 Yong An Li

DURTY NELLIE'S (YY)

Regarded mainly as a bar, Nellie's serves up excellent soups and sandwiches. The fries are crispy and thin; the salads loaded with cheese and meat. Expect big servings.
✚ M3 ✉ 12a Dong Guiao Xiejie, Chaoyang District ☎ 6502 2802 ◉ 5pm–late 🚌 115, 11

THE ELEPHANT (Y)

This restaurant has been going since 1996. It isn't trendy but is always packed because of the filling, hearty, home-cooked Russian food. Don't miss the potato *latke* (pancakes) or the pickled herring. A clue that it's the real McCoy—the local Russian expatriate community eats here.
✚ L6 ✉ 17 Ritan Beilu, Chaoyang District ◉ 11.30am–2am 🚌 28, 43

JUSTINE'S (YYY)

One of Beijing's most established Continental restaurants and an excellent choice for Sunday brunch. The main courses lean toward French cuisine but it's nothing fancy, just solid, consistent, moderately expensive Western food.

✚ L7 ✉ 1F Jianguo Hotel, 5 Jianguomenwai Dajie, Chaoyang District ☎ 6500 2233, ext 8039 🕐 noon–2.30, 6–10.30 🚇 Yong An Li

MEXICAN WAVE (YY)

Margaritas and beer imported from Mexico make an appropriate prelude to the pizzas, quesadillas, burritos, burgers and huge salads. Near the corner of Guanghua Lu.

✚ M6 ✉ Dongdaqiao Lu, Chaoyang District ☎ 6506 3961 🕐 10am–2am 🚌 28, 403

MOSCOW (Y–YY)

The reason to come here now is to dine surrounded by faded elegance, under chandeliers and amid fluted columns. While the spicy borscht is still worth ordering, some dishes can be disappointing. Try steak with mushroom sauce or the chicken curry drumsticks.

✚ C3 ✉ 135 Xizhimenwai Dajie, Xicheng District (access by a small road on the west side of the Beijing Exhibition Center; look for *Mockba Pectopan* a short walk down on the right) ☎ 6835 4454 🕐 11–2, 5–9 🚇 Xizhimen

POWER HOUSE (YY)

Photographs on the menu here show standard items like spaghetti bolognese, pork chops and burgers. Live music at night keeps things buzzing. Close to the Sanlitun area.

✚ N4 ✉ 35 Xaaoyun Lu, Chaoyang District ☎ 8454 1975 🕐 11am–3am 🚌 113, 117

ROYAL CAFE (YY–YYY)

For fresh Norwegian salmon and other Scandinavian specialties, try the restaurant in the Radisson SAS Hotel in the northeast of the city (► 86). Beef is regularly flown in, and the Sunday brunch is luxurious and consistently good.

✚ Just north of M1 ✉ 3 Beisanhuandong Lu, Chaoyang District ☎ 6466 3388 🕐 11–10 🚌 302, 379

STEAK AND EGGGS (YY)

No-frills American cooking is the specialty of this popular diner tucked behind the Friendship Store. The portions are generous and the prices realistic. Head here for Sunday brunch—if you can find a table.

✚ L6 ✉ 5 Xiushuinan Jie, Juanguomenwai, Chaoyang District ☎ 6592 8088 🕐 Mon–Fri 7.30am–10.30pm, Sat–Sun 7.30am–midnight 🚇 Jianguomen

VINCENT CAFÉ (Y)

This newcomer to the Beijing culinary scene specializes in trditional Breton cooking, with crepes and galettes (savory buckwheat pancakes) to the fore. There's a beguiling choice of fillings and flavors to choose from and sweet Breton cider to drink. Outdoor seating on the patio in summer.

✚ Off map, east of the Capital Airport Expressway ✉ 2 Jiuxiangqiao Lu (to the rear of the Dashanzi art galleries), Chaoyang District ☎ 8456 4823 🕐 11–11 🚌 403, 404

FAST FOOD

Nearly all major franchised fast-food restaurants are adding outlets in and around Beijing: A&W, Baskin Robbins, Dunkin' Donuts, KFC, McDonald's, Pizza Hut, Subway and TGI Friday's. A stretch of Jianguomenwai Dajie, the area around Zhengyangmen (Qianmen Gate ► 44) and Wangfujing Dajie (► 61), are the places to find out how American fast food translates in a decidedly Chinese setting. KFC has added Beijing duck to its menu!

71

Antiques & Crafts

EXPORTING ANTIQUES

Chinese authorities classify any item made before 1949 as an antique. The export of any such item must be approved by the Beijing Cultural Relics Bureau. Approval takes the form of a red wax seal and an official receipt; any genuine antiques dealer should be able to show you this. As the vast majority of 'antiques' are really reproductions, the need for export approval does not arise very often. If you buy an antique that lacks the seal, you can have it verified and approved at the Friendship Store (☎ 6401 4608 for an appointment) every Monday afternoon. Packing and shipping are not generally available, and credit cards are accepted only at larger, modern stores.

BEIJING CURIO CITY

This large mall has over 200 stalls selling a wide range of items from bric-à-brac to genuine antiques. The best time to visit is on Sunday morning, when vendors set up shop in the surrounding streets.

✚ Off the map, southwest of the city ✉ 21 Dongsanhuan Nan Lu, west of Huawei Bridge ☎ 6774 7711 ⏰ 9.30–6.30

CHAOWAI MARKET

Two large warehouses at the end of a small lane are stuffed with antique objects of desire: medicine cabinets, chests, first-class reproductions of Qing and Ming furniture, ceramics, Mao memorabilia, jewelry and other knick-knacks. A visit is vital for anyone thinking of buying a piece of furniture or a quality *objet d'art*. Packing and shipping are easily arranged. Serious bargaining is essential. Try to end up paying less than half the price first quoted.

✚ L5 ✉ Shichangie, Chaoyangmenwai Dajie, Chaoyang District ⏰ 9–6 🚇 Chaoyangmen

HONGQIAO MARKET

Seek out the antiques shops on the third floor—easy to miss, tucked away behind the pearl stalls (▶ 75). A lot of the merchandise is reproduction, but some of the furniture is small enough to be portable and the temple plaques are appealing. Shop No. 6 specializes in old clocks. Bear in mind when bargaining that these

stores sell primarily to tourists.

✚ J9 ✉ 36 Hongqiao Lu, Chongwen District ☎ 6713 3354/6711 7429 ⏰ 9–6 🚌 36, 39, 43

HUAXIA ARTS & CRAFTS BRANCH STORE

The second floor of this government store retails clocks, pocket watches, rugs, chinaware and woodcarvings from temples. Be aware most of them are probably fake, but at least they look authentic.

✚ F8 ✉ 122 Liulichangdong Jie, Xuanwu District ☎ 6513 6204 ⏰ 9–7 🚇 Qianmen

LANYATANG ANTIQUES

This store sells genuine antiques and curios from all over China, everything from carpets, paintings and wooden cabinets to statuettes and jade ornaments. In the same line of shops as Beijing Fine Jewelers (▶ 74).

✚ M4 ✉ 6A Gongrentiyuchangdong Lu (aka Gongti Dong Lu), Chaoyang District ☎ 6502 1627 ⏰ 10–8 🚌 115, 118

LIANGMAHE MARKET

In an arcade opposite the Kempinski Hotel, some 50 small stores sell pottery, paintings, old watches and antique furniture. One or two of the furniture dealers have a larger stock in their warehouses and will happily take potential customers there to view. However, there is a high mark-up, and you'll pay a reasonable price only after serious bargaining.

➕ N2 ✉ 49 Liangmaqiao Lu, Chaoyang District 🕐 9–9 🚇 9, 300, 402, 801

LIULICHANG JIE

Conveniently located southwest of Qianmen, this famous old street—now renovated to look its age—is well worth a visit even if you buy nothing. Fine antiques stores stock woodblock print reproductions, porcelain, jade, snuff bottles, paintings and a very few genuine antique pieces. Worth considering are the rubbings of bas-relief carvings taken off ancient temples and tombs. A number of the larger stores are government-owned; bargaining in this area is limited.

➕ F8 ✉ Liulichangdong Jie, Xuanwu District 🕐 9–6 🚇 Qianmen

PANJIAYUAN MARKET

Come here early on weekends, especially Sundays; by afternoon this market is already winding down. Most of the 'antiques' are fake, but they are quality fakes and gratifying purchases may be made if you bargain rigorously. Never pay anything like the first price quoted. It is best to arrive by taxi, but make sure the taxi driver doesn't just drop you by the stalls selling worthless bric-à-brac—ask your hotel to specify in writing that you want to go to the antiques part of the market.

➕ M10 ✉ Huawei Lu Dajie, Dongsanhuan, Chaoyang District 🕐 8–1 🚇 35, 41

QIANMEN CARPET

This is one of the largest antique carpet dealers in Beijing. There are some very expensive antique carpets from Xinjiang and Tibet, as well as hand-made imitations and Henan silk carpets—the objectives of most visitors. The showroom is a converted air-raid shelter dating from the 1960s.

➕ K9 ✉ 59 Xingfu Dajie, Chongwen District ☎ 6715 1687 🕐 9.30–5.30 🚇 6, 35, 51, 60

SHARD BOX STORE

Come here and you will be instantly won over by these highly original jewelry boxes made from wood, silver and ivory, and ingeniously decorated with shards of porcelain from broken vases. The prices are equally attractive.

➕ L6 ✉ 1 Ritanbei Lu, Chaoyang District ☎ 8561 3712 🕐 9–7 🚇 29, 908

TIBET SHOP

The specialty of this small store is hand-woven Tibetan rugs, beautifully ornamented with religious and other symbols. Most are reproductions. Tibetan bone, amber and agate necklaces are also available.

➕ M4 ✉ Bei Sanlitun Nanli (just off Xindong Lu), Chaoyang District ☎ 6417 5963 🕐 10–8.30 🚇 115, 118

SPOTTING FAKES

Check the bottoms and insides of antiques for clues about the antiquity—made-yesterday immitations are rarely finished on the underside of a drawer, for example, so you'll be able to spot the new ply wood. Inspect seams and search for extra buttons (a luxury that real designers provide, but knock-off manufacturers neglect). If you can tell the real McCoy from a fake, the sales clerk will be able to tell you're the real McCoy too—and will be more likely to quote you the right price.

Arts & Souvenirs

CERAMICS

The history of ceramics in China is as old as the civilization itself. The technology and art of design evolved from neolithic times, through the Bronze Age and all the great dynasties from the 6th century onwards. The Ming dynasty produced some of the most beautiful work through the use of under-glaze blue-and-white painting.

ARTS & CRAFT STORE

This store in the prestigious China World Trade Center retails fine china, carpets and an array of expensive *objets d'art*, and has its own foreign exchange counter.

✚ N7 ✉ 1 Jianguomenwai Dajie, Chaoyang District ☎ 6505 2261 ⏰ 9.20am–9.40pm 🚌 1, 4, 37

BEIJING ARTS & CRAFT CENTRAL STORE

This huge emporium, conveniently situated on Beijing's main shopping street, is famous for its (expensive) jade, but you'll also find gold and silver jewelry, glassware, stone and wood carving, cloisonné, lacquer, art materials and seals.

✚ H6 ✉ 200 Wangfujing Dajie, Dongcheng District ☎ 6528 8866 ⏰ 9am–10pm 🚇 Wangfujing

BEIJING FINE JEWELERS

Ex-pats swear by this Sanlitun outlet with its great selection of gold, silver and other jewelry. If you have a favorite bangle, bring a photo of it and they will reproduce it.

✚ M4 ✉ 6A Gongrentiyuchangdong Lu (aka Gongti Dong Lu), Chaoyang District ☎ 6592 7118 ⏰ 9.30–7 🚌 115, 118

BEIJING JADE CARVING FACTORY

The wide selection of jadeware here ranges from magnificently ponderous examples of this renowned Chinese handicraft to the more luggage-friendly in size. Look carefully at some of the finer items, noticing how cleverly the differing shades of green are used.

✚ L9 ✉ 11 Guangming Lu, Chongwen District ☎ 6702 7371 ⏰ 9–5 🚇 Jianguomen

FORBIDDEN CITY SHOPS

Small shops inside the Forbidden City include a stall at the entrance to the Gate of Supreme Harmony that sells an inexpensive and attractive poster map of the palace complex. The most useful gift shop, simply called Gift Shop, just inside the north gate (where the rented audiotapes are returned), has a small but discriminating selection of art books, quality reproductions of Ming and Qing art, CDs, puzzles, theme umbrellas and other souvenirs. Next door, the bookstore with the grandiose title Books of Cultural Relics, Archaeology & Arts has the city's best selection of translated academic titles on Chinese art and archeology. Other arts and crafts stores form a shopping corridor where you'll find affordable gifts.

✚ G5 ✉ Jingshanqian Jie, Dongcheng District ⏰ 8.30–5 🚇 Qianmen

FRIENDSHIP STORE

The store is worth a visit, if only to check the fixed prices and the range of items. There are four levels; all but the second floor, where there is a foreign-exchange facility at a branch of the Bank of China, offer a good range of arts and crafts: jade, porcelain, cloisonné, lacquerware, silk, linen, paintings, carpets, works of calligraphy and kites.

➕ L7 ✉ 17 Jianguomenwai Dajie, Chaoyang District ☎ 6500 3311 🕐 9.30–8.30 🚌 1, 2, 3, 4, 9, 802

HONGQIAO MARKET

In the central area on the third floor, freshwater pearls are made up on the spot to customers' wishes. There are no fixed prices, so bargaining is required. Experts rub two pearls together; the rougher the contact the better; if they rub together smoothly the pearls are of poorer quality. Arts and crafts stores share the same floor: Nos. 213–14 and 218 specialize in cloisonné (▶ 18); No. 219 is devoted to finely crafted gilded-silver ornaments. Another area is devoted to antiques (▶ 72–73).

➕ J9 ✉ Tiantan Lu, Chongwen District 🕐 9–6 🚌 36, 39, 43

HONGSHENG MUSICAL INSTRUMENTS

This musical instruments hall is on the first floor of the Shengdongtang Department Store. In addition to guitars and small brass instruments, there is a selection of traditional Chinese instruments, which are not easy to find outside China. Also visit No. 221 in the Lisheng Shopping Mall (☎ 6525 6255).

➕ H6 ✉ 225 Wangfujing Dajie, Dongcheng District ☎ 6513 5190 🕐 9.30am–11pm 🚌 104, 103, 803

LUFTHANSA CENTER

The fifth floor of this large shopping plaza is devoted to arts and crafts and offers a wide choice of jade, pottery and porcelain, and assorted collectibles. A separate room serves as a gallery for Chinese prints. Prices are fixed, but a 10 percent discount is still worth trying for.

➕ N2 ✉ 50 Liangmaqiao Lu, Chaoyang District ☎ 6465 3388 🕐 9–9 🚌 300, 402, 801

SCROLL ALLEY

Although way off the beaten track, this motley street market is easy to reach by subway. Walk east from Chegong-zhuang station, turning north when you see the stalls on your left. A good place to have pictures mounted as scrolls.

➕ D3/4 ✉ North of Ping'anlixi Dajie 🕐 9–5 🚇 Chegongzhuang

YONGHEGONG DAJIE

On the way to the Lama Temple you'll see this row of shops specializing in Buddhist religious paraphernalia—candles, incense sticks, statuettes, mahogany shrines, prayer cushions, prayer wheels; the choice is almost overwhelming.

➕ J2 ✉ Yonghegong Dajie, Chaoyang District 🕐 8–7 🚇 Yonghegong

OLD PEKING

Two books first written in the 1930s by foreigners living in the city provide an insight into the old capital and its way of life. They are *Peking*, by Juliet Bredon and *In Search of Old Peking*, by Arlington & Lewisohn (both published by Oxford University Press). *Twilight in the Forbidden City*, written by Reginald Johnston, English tutor and tennis coach to the last emperor, Puyi, has also been republished by Oxford University Press.

Clothing

BARGAINING

In Sanlitun and the Silk Market there are no fixed prices and bargaining is the rule. In general, try to bring down the vendor's first asking price before committing yourself to an offer and remember that you will always need to settle at a price above your first offer. A pair of Armani jeans should go for around 100 yuan, Caterpillar boots or a Gore-Tex jacket for around twice that.

ERMENEGILDO ZEGNA

This exclusive designer-clothing boutique is typical of the stores in the elegant Peninsula Palace Hotel. Its neighbors include Versace and Boss. The prices are often higher than those in Europe, but wealthy Chinese customers have been known to turn up here with suitcases stuffed with cash and blow huge sums on only a few garments.

J6 ⊠ 8 Jinyu Hutong, Dongcheng District ☎ 6559 2888 ⏰ 10.30–9.30 🚌 110, 116, 120, 204

FRIENDSHIP STORE

You'll find clothing on the second floor. There is a terrific choice of silk by the yard, and the selection of traditional Chinese dress is worth a look. Come here and check the prices before trying your hand at bargaining in street markets.

L7 ⊠ 17 Jianguomenwai Dajie, Chaoyang District ☎ 6500 3311 ⏰ 9.30–8.30 🚌 1, 2, 3, 4, 9, 802

GANJIAKOU

This market attracts few tourists because the clothes are entirely Asian in style, but it will appeal to those interested in investigating the latest fashions from Taiwan and Korea. Stalls line the street, Sanlihe Lu, as far as Baiwanzhuangxi Lu. As usual in this type of market, bargaining is essential.

B4 ⊠ Sanlihe Lu, Haidian District ⏰ 9–5 🚌 102, 103, 114

HUFANG LU

Merchandise turns over quickly in this street market of busy clothing stalls, but European and North American visitors may well find most of the garments unfashionable. However, prices are reasonable and occasionally worthwhile silk items turn up. Bargaining is essential.

F8 ⊠ Hufang Lu, Xuanwu District ⏰ 9–5 🚌 6, 14, 15

MILITARY SUPPLIES

This place, not far from the Jing Guang Center, stocks garments and gear of the People's Liberation Army (PLA), including heavy, double-breasted coats with gold buttons and PLA caps complete with red star.

N6 ⊠ 23 Dongsanhuanbei Lu, Chaoyang District ⏰ 9–5.30 🚌 9, 13, 117, 350, 402, 405, 801

RUIFUXIANG SILK AND CLOTH STORE

The area around Dazhalan Jie (▶ 60)—a beehive of commercial activity for five centuries—is home to a number of interesting old stores, including the well-known Ruifuxiang, with its distinctive arched entrance and its facade decorated with storks. Raw silk, the main draw here, comes in a dazzling choice of colors, textures and patterns.

G8 ⊠ 5 Qianmen Dazhalan Jie, Xuanwu District ☎ 6303 5315 ⏰ 9am–10pm 🚇 Qianmen

RUSSIAN MARKET

This is the unofficial name for the clothing market

that starts halfway up Ritan Lu and continues around the corner into Yabao Lu. Everything is geared toward the many Russian shoppers who arrive in Beijing on the Trans-Siberian railway with empty bags and return carrying or wearing as much as is humanly possible. Fur coats are a big draw—sable, mink, rabbit and fox—but there is also a fair selection of gloves, belts, scarves, women's garments and assorted other clothing items. The familiar designer names are not seen here, and the styles may seem garish to Western shoppers, but there are bargains to be had. However, the vendors like to sell in bulk and may ask how many identical items you are interested in buying.

➕ L6 ✉ Ritan Lu and Yabao Lu, Chaoyang District ⏰ 9–dusk 🚇 Jianguomen

SANLITUN LU

Silk Market is by far the best known place for designer clothes, but a visit to Sanlitun Lu (➤ 61) may well prove equally gratifying. As the stalls are mainly on one side of Sanlitunbeijielu, there is more space for walking, looking and trying on. The atmosphere is less hectic than the Silk Market, and often, better prices can be negotiated. The bulk of the merchandise consists of designer-label jeans, shirts and women's wear. A couple of stalls sell shoes and, at the far end where

wicker furniture is sold, the stores continue around the corner to a fruit and vegetable market.

➕ M3 ✉ Off Sanlitun Lu, Chaoyang District ⏰ 9–7 🚌 115, 118

SILK MARKET

A visit to this crowded market may convince you that very few visitors leave Beijing without having purchased a designer-label item of clothing or something in silk at a fraction of the store price. Silk Market is a small lane, off Xiushuidong Jie, crammed with stalls on both its sides. Shoppers, mostly visitors and expatriates, but many Beijingers too, fill every space and at times the atmosphere can seem frenzied. Apart from silk and cashmere, available at phenomenally low prices, bargains are to be had in Gore-Tex and down jackets, as well as shirts, sweaters, raincoats, shoes and patchwork quilts. Famous brand names sit alongside impressive fakes and factory seconds. Be on your guard, and always check for imperfections.

➕ M6/7 ✉ Xiushuidong Jie, Chaoyang District ⏰ 10–dusk 🚇 Jianguomen

YUANLONG SILK CORPORATION LTD

This is one of the oldest silk stores in Beijing, easy to find near the north entrance of Tiantan Park. A tailoring service is available

➕ H9 ✉ 55 Tiantan Lu, Chongwen District ☎ 6701 2854 ⏰ 9–5 🚌 34, 35, 36

SILK

Gorgeously embroidered silk shirts, blouses, lingerie and bedspreads make ideal gifts. The Silk Market and the Friendship Store are both good hunting grounds, along with the large government-owned Beijing Silk Corporation, near the south gate of the Temple of Heaven. Bear in mind, though, that many items of silk clothing that seem such good value will never be the same after cleaning, even dry cleaning.

Department Stores & Shopping Centers

SHOPPING

Beijing's social revolution is nowhere more apparent than in the changed shopping scene. It is still possible to come across old state-owned stores whose surly staff give the clear impression that they don't want to be bothered by a troublesome customer with the audacity to wish to buy something. However, market forces are rapidly transforming everything, from store design inside and out, down to the new-minted smiles on the faces of helpful assistants. Most important, the shelves are now stocked with quality foreign-made goods and consumer items that were unknown a decade ago.

BEIJING DEPARTMENT STORE

It seems hard to believe that this store has survived so long in this prestigious location in competition with Sun Dong An Plaza (► below). A little more than 12 years ago, this was Beijing's showpiece department store but now, upstaged by Beijing's newly arrived array of huge, smart shopping malls, its amateurish displays and general drabness puts it on a par with a cast-off statue of Lenin. See it while it lasts.
✚ H6 ✉ 255 Wangfujing Dajie, Doncheng District ☎ 6512 6677 ⏰ 8.30–8.30 🚌 104, 103

CHINA WORLD TRADE SHOPPING CENTER

Chairman Mao would be appalled by this monument to yuppie consumerism. Among the chic boutiques and lifestyle stores is a well-stocked Arts and Craft Store (► 74), a useful deli, a drugstore and a large branch of the Hong Kong supermarket chain, Wellcome, which stocks an excellent range of local and Western foods.
✚ N7 ✉ 1 Jianguomenwai Dajie, Chaoyang District ☎ 6505 2288 ⏰ 9.30–9.30 Ⓜ Guomao 🚌 1, 4, 37, 52

KERRY CENTER

Though smaller and less exclusive than China World (above), this mall contains an excellent range of shops, from boutiques and hairdressers to aromatherapy stores and wine retailers.
✚ M6 ✉ 1 Guang Hua Lu, Chaoyang District ☎ 6561 8833 ⏰ 9–9 🚌 48, 908

LUFTHANSA CENTER

This very large center houses one of Beijing's best supermarkets. A number of pleasant restaurants and cafés in the vicinity sustain weary shoppers.
✚ N2 ✉ 50 Liangmaqiao Lu, Chaoyang District ☎ 6465 1188 ⏰ 10–10 🚌 300, 402, 801

PACIFIC CENTURY PLACE

An office and residential complex containing the useful Pacific Department Store. Stocking top brands, you'll find a supermarket in the basement, perfumes on the first floor, men's and women's clothing on the third and fourth and DVDs and electrical goods at the top of the building.
✚ N4 ✉ 2A Gongrentiyuchangbei Lu (aka Gongti Bei Lu), Chaoyang District ☎ 6539 3888 ⏰ 10–10 🚌 115, 118

SUN DONG AN PLAZA

This is the big one, the glitzy flagship of the renowned and revamped Wangfujing. The 11-story plaza with three basement levels opened in 1998. Its huge floor space includes department stores, clothing outlets, an eight-screen cineplex, food court, restaurants and an entertainment center.
✚ H5 ✉ 138 Wangfujing Dajie, Dongcheng District ☎ 6527 6688 ⏰ 9–10 🚌 104, 103

Curios, Carpets & Computers

FOREIGN LANGUAGES BOOKSTORE

At one time this was Beijing's only store selling publications in English and other foreign languages. It still has the largest stock of such books in the city. As well as books and tapes in English and other languages, a range of dictionaries and other reference material is available in the Foreign Language Reference Bookstore at No. 219 Wangfujing (entrance through the Dunkin' Donuts shop).

🖪 H6 ⬜ 235 Wangfujing Dajie, Dongcheng District ☎ 6512 6903 ⏰ 9–9 🚇 Wangfujing 🚌 104, 211

HUATAI SILK CARPETS

This factory, one of the most famous in China, has been producing exquisite handmade silk carpets since 1915. The quality of the silk ensures that no carpet will fade or alter in appearnce for at least a century.

🖪 L2 ⬜ Room 7 (1st floor) Golden Tower, Chaoyang District ☎ 6440 2121 ⏰ 9–7.30 🚇 Donghimen

SOUVENIR & BRIC-À-BRAC MARKET

A useful row of stalls near the Peace Hotel sells inexpensive Chinese gifts and mementos that make good souvenirs. Copies of the *Little Red Book* are originals from the Cultural Revolution, while the glitzy watches and musical lighters bearing the face of Mao have been produced recently.

🖪 J6 ⬜ Jinyu Hutong, Dongcheng District ⏰ 10–dusk 🚌 104, 106

STAMP MARKET

Asian stamps—some rare—as well as postcards and phone cards are on sale, and there are usually some stalls dealing in coins, including the old bronze ones with holes in the middle.

🖪 Off the map ⬜ Funite Furniture City, Beisihuanzhong Jie ⏰ 9–5 🚌 302

TIANTAN PARK MARKET

A covered corridor near the park's east entrance is filled with stalls displaying bric-à-brac and fascinating cultural curios from the 1960s. Look out for the ubiquitous Maoist clocks depicting revolutionary peasants holding aloft the *Little Red Book*.

🖪 J9 ⬜ East side of Tiantan Park, Chongwen District ⏰ 9–5.30 🚌 6, 15, 17, 20, 35, 39, 43, 106

ZHONGGUANCUN

Computer stores are concentrated here in the northwest of the city. (From Xizhimen subway station take a minibus along Baishiqiao Lu.) You will see the stores a couple of stops past the Friendship Hotel. A wide range of hardware, peripherals and software (beware—some is pirated) is available.

🖪 Off the map, north of A1 ⬜ Haidian Jie, Haidian District ⏰ 9–5 🚌 301, 303, 332, 333

BEIJING BOOKS

The *Beijing Scene* guidebook (scene@well.com) is compiled by a group of expatriates (⬜ Beijing Scene Publishing, 400 Main St., Ansonia, CT 06401, USA) and is well worth dipping into for its wealth of informed and practical information. *The Forbidden City* by Mary Holdsworth and Caroline Courtauld (1995, Odyssey Press) is the most attractively produced book on its subject. *From Emperor to Citizen* (1987, Oxford University Press) is the autobiography of Puyi, the last emperor, who lived in the Forbidden City until 1924. Good places to buy books on Beijing include the gift stores in the five-star hotels, notably the Swissotel (➤ 86), the Foreign Languages Bookstore (➤ this page) and two stores inside the north gate of the Forbidden City (➤ 74).

Bars & Licensed Cafés

A FAST-CHANGING SCENE

Informal restaurants during the day and early evening, Beijing's licensed cafés gradually transform themselves into bars as the night goes on. Always call before heading off for the night—don't forget to ask your hotel to write down the name and address in Chinese for the benefit of taxi drivers.

BIG EASY BAR AND GRILL

Cajun in Beijing may be hard to wrap your brain around but this bar brings over international singers, so the jazz and blues alone draws in the crowds.

✚ Off map ✉ Chaoyang Park south gate, just off Nongzhanguan Nanlu, Chaoyang District ☎ 6508 6776 🕐 5pm–2am 🚌 115, 118

BLUE HAND

This little bar opposite the Kempinski Hotel is frequented by expatriates and foreign students who value the inexpensive beer and food. On warm summer nights, the outdoor seating is an added attraction.

✚ N2 ✉ Liangmaqiao Lu, Chaoyang District 🕐 24 hours 🚌 300, 402, 801

CENTRO

Currently a very popular nightspot in the Kerry Center (► 78) , Centro is a giant cocktail bar and lounge with a private room and wine cellars. The happy hour and friendly waiters add to its appeal.

✚ M6 ✉ 1/F Kerry Center Hotel, 1 Guanghua Lu, Chaoyang District ☎ 6561 8833 🕐 24 hours 🚌 48, 908

CHAMPAGNE BAR

One of the better hotel bars in Beijing. The resident band, typically Filipino, jump-starts the evening around 7.30, after happy hour, and continues until 1am. Reservations are available.

✚ N5 ✉ Jing Guang Centre, Dongsanhuanbei Lu, Chaoyang District ☎ 6597 8888 ext. 2561 🕐 4pm–1am 🚌 112, 113, 9, 402

CLUB FOOTBALL CENTER

Inside the Red House Hotel, this bar has a real pub atmosphere, at least when they're screening British and European soccer matches, or NBA (US basketball) and NFL (US football) games. Work off those extra calories playing pool, table football or darts. Food available.

✚ L3 ✉ 10 Chunxiu Lu, Chaoyang District ☎ 6416 7786 🕐 11am–midnight 🚌 117

CLUB LOOK

The latest nightspot from the Henry Lee stable (► 24) is a huge affair comprising a dining room and two bars, where the resident DJs play mainly hip hop.

✚ N4 ✉ Gongrentiyuchangbei Lu (aka Gongti Bei Lu, first *hutong* on the right after Sanlitun Lu), Chaoyang District ☎ 6506 6770 🕐 8.30pm–late 🚌 115, 118

COCO CLUB

Latin American music and food sets the scene in this comfortable hotel bar. Early in the evening you can enjoy a game of darts or a quiet conversation, but when the band starts up, just sit back and enjoy the show.

✚ H5 ✉ Prime Hotel, 2 Wangfujing Dajie, Dongcheng District ☎ 6513 6666 🕐 6pm–1.30am 🚌 104, 111

THE DEN

The former Owl Pen has

had a makeover with a street-level bar and second-floor disco where DJs play mainly pop and R and B. You'll find the entrance next to the City Hotel.

✚ M4

✉ 4 Gongrentiyuchangdong Lu (aka Gongti Dong Lu), Chaoyang District ☎ 6592 6290

🕐 Sun–Thu 10.30am–3am, Fri–Sat 10.30–6am 🚌 104, 111

DURTY NELLIE'S

This Irish pub, where Guinness is on tap, is a favorite hangout for locals and expats. Cover bands often play modern pop and rock music .

✚ M3 ✉ 12A Dongdaqiao Xiejie, Chaoyang District ☎ 6502 2802

🕐 5.30pm–1.30am 🚌 118

FRANK'S PLACE

One of the first bars in the Sanlitun area, this remains a firm favorite with regulars. It's a good place to catch an international sports event on television.

✚ M4 ✉ Gongti Donglu, Chaoyang District (200 yards/ 200m) south of City Hotel) ☎ 6507 2617 🕐 11.30am– 1.30am 🚌 120, 117

GOOSE & DUCK

A passable imitation of an English pub, with Bass ale from the barrel. There is live music most nights.

✚ L6 ✉ 1 Bihuju Nanlu, Chaoyang District ☎ 6538 1691 🕐 24 hours

🚇 Dongsishitiao, then bus 115

HALF & HALF

While open

homosexuality is not as acceptable in Beijing as in some other cities, a few gay bars are emerging and lasting on the nightlife scene. This is one of the most popular and one of the oldest gay bars.

✚ M3 ✉ 15 Sanlitun Nanli, Chaoyang District ☎ 6416 6919 🕐 Noon–2am 🚌 113, 115

HIDDEN TREE

If you are looking for ales, such as Dyvel or Hoegaarden, you will find them in this packed pub where local bands perform on weekends.

✚ M6 ✉ 12 Dongdaqiao, Xiejie, Chaoyang District ☎ 6509 3642 🕐 Mon–Sat 11am–late; Sun 1pm–late 🚌 117, 120

JACK AND JILL BAR

This friendly bar is typical of the new breed of bar opening in the Sanlitun area. The decor is bright and cheerful and the staff anxious to please. A pleasant place to relax in the evening after a shopping trip.

✚ M3 ✉ 52 Sanlitun Lu, Chaoyang District ☎ 6416 4697 🕐 6pm–late 🚌 115, 118

JAZZ YA

One of the best cocktail menus in this part of town draws local yuppies and expatriates from around the globe. The food is Western, while the jazz is international.

✚ M3 ✉ 18 Sanlitun Lu, Chaoyang District ☎ 6415 1227 🕐 10.30am–2am 🚌 115, 118

BAR HOPPING

The Sanlitun Lu area is the only part of Beijing where you can bar-hop on foot. In addition to the establishments mentioned on these pages, there are a host of other places in the vicinity. The small *hutongs* between Gongrentiyuchangdong Lu and Nansanlitun Lu (✚ M4) are alight with neon at night and more bars cluster behind the Swing bar at No. 58 farther up Sanlitun Lu.

BEIJING INTERNET

The Beijing cyber scene has never been the same since the evening in June 2002 when four local teenagers set fire to an internet café in the Haidan District, causing the deaths of 24 people. The government's response was to close down more than 2,400 unlicensed premises, few of which were ever allowed to reopen. Today's cyber cafés are carefully regulated and few in number. At On/Off bar and restaurant, you can surf the net to your heart's content while listening to good music (🚇 M3 ✉ 5 Xingfu Yicun Xili (off Xingfucunzhong Lu), Chaoyang District ☎ 6415 8083 🕐 7pm–2am).

JOHN BULL PUB

Brass fittings, dark wood and British Empire memorabilia—brass wallplates and Toby jugs—complement fish and chips and Yorkshire pudding in this mock-English pub. The first pub in Beijing to serve Guinness, John Bull and Tetley's bitter on draft. Tuesday is quiz night.

🚇 L6 ✉ 44 Guanghua Lu, Chaoyang District ☎ 6532 5905 🕐 9am–midnight
🚌 1, 4, 9, 802

MINDER CAFÉ

All the ingredients for a good night out: Decent bar food, live music, no cover and a comfortable, spacious area to relax after a day's sightseeing.

🚇 M4 ✉ Dongdaqiao Xiejie Nansanlitun, Chaoyang District ☎ 6500 6066 🕐 6pm–2am
🚌 115

NASHVILLE

This country-and-western bar has live music most nights—'down-home' folks having a good time. Happy hour 5–8.

🚇 M4 ✉ Dongdaqiaoxie Jie, Nansanlitun, Chaoyang District ☎ 6502 4201 🕐 6pm–2am
🚌 115

PUBLIC SPACE

With its air of relaxed informality and tables on the sidewalk, this typical Sanlitun bar is buoyantly decorated and stays open until dawn if demand warrants.

🚇 M3 ✉ 50 Sanlitun Lu, Chaoyang District ☎ 6416 0759 🕐 10am–2am
🚌 115, 18

SCHILLER'S

This bar opposite the Kempinski Hotel has a reputation among the expatriate community and locals alike for friendly service and relaxed atmosphere. You can also get a meal here and there are a few tables outdoors.

🚇 N2 ✉ Liangmaqiao Lu, Chaoyang District ☎ 6461 9276 🕐 11.30am–12.30am
🚌 300, 402, 801

WAITING FOR GODOT

A literary café that is the brainchild of Zhao Liao, a Beijing intellectual with a passion for the theater. Sip a coffee or choose from the quirky beer menu—Chimay, Kwak, Leffe, Moretti—while looking over the collection of unusual CDs and art books or admiring the prints and posters decorating the walls.

🚇 H3 ✉ 24 Building 14 Jiaodaokou Dongdajie, Xicheng District ☎ 6407 3093 🕐 10–10 🚌 Dongzhimen, then bus 18, 24

WHAT? BAR

Pop fans squeeze into this tiny bar space to watch the local rock bands perform. Listen in while enjoying what must be some of the cheapest drinks in the city.

🚇 G5 ✉ D72 Beichang Jie (north of west gate of Forbidden City), Xicheng District ☎ No phone 🕐 8pm–Late 🚌 5

Clubs & Discos

BLACK ROSE

The best hotel disco in the city, with live bands.
➕ Off the map ✉ Holiday Inn Lido, Jichang Lu, Jiangtai Lu, Chaoyang District ☎ 6437 6297 ⏰ 5pm–2am (3.30am at weekends) 🚌 401, 403

CD CAFÉ JAZZ CLUB

The archetypal jazz club, smoky and dim, where you can relax and observe the city from an outdoor patio. Live musicians appear Wednesday to Sunday (small cover charge).
➕ N3 ✉ Dongsanhuanbei Lu, Chaoyang District (southwest of Museum of Agriculture)
☎ 6506 8288 ⏰ Daily 4pm–2am 🚌 300, 402, 801

HARD ROCK CAFÉ

Rock memorabilia, pricey drinks and tasty barbecued pork chops and grilled fajitas. A resident band plays short sessions after 9pm, except Sunday, when there is a disco (cover charge).
➕ N2 ✉ 8 Dongsanhuanbei Lu, Chaoyang District (next to Great Wall Sheraton Hotel)
☎ 6590 6688 ⏰ Sun–Thu 11.30pm–2am (3am at weekends) 🚌 300, 402, 801

NIGHTMAN DISCO

Only a few years ago, dance clubs were unknown in China, so although the Nightman may seem a little unsophisticated, it is still remarkable how exuberantly Beijingers have warmed to the genre.
➕ M1 ✉ 2 Xibahenan Lu (opposite west gate of International Exhibition Center), Chaoyang District ☎ 6466 2562 ⏰ 8.30pm–5am 🚌 302, 379, 18

ORANGE (JU ZI)

This hip dance club tends to attract the twenty-somethings who weren't born when the 1970s decor first hit the scene. If you are looking for techno, trance and house, this is the spot to blow your eardrums. Orange is also a great place to people-watch the lollipop-sucking barely older-than-teen crowd who have co-opted Western cultural styles.
➕ M4 ✉ 2–10 Xingfu Yicun (along an alley north of Worker's Stadium) Chaoyang District
☎ 6415 7413 ⏰ Mon–Thu 9pm–3am 🚌 117, 120

SAN WEI BOOKSTORE

The floor above the bookselling area is a teahouse by day and a buzzing bar at night. The unusual decor suits the music, usually either live classical Chinese fare or laid-back jazz. Well worth a visit for the cultural experience.
➕ E7 ✉ 60 Fuxingmennei Dajie, Xicheng District (opposite Minzu Hotel) ☎ 6601 3204
⏰ 9.30am–10.30pm 🚇 Fuxingmen

THE CLUB

Techno and house dance club, which is popular among businessmen, expats and students. If that is not your scene, try the lounge upstairs.
➕ M3 ✉ 43 Bei Sanlitun, off Sanlitun Bar Street, Chaoyang District ☎ 6416 1077
⏰ 10pm–4am 🚌 115, 118

FOOD, DRINK, AND CULTURE

From around 10.30am on Sunday mornings at the Jianguo Hotel (➕ M7) on Jianguomenwai Dajie, a small classical orchestra provides a backdrop for a relaxing drink or meal. The atmosphere is pleasant, despite the setting in a hotel foyer, and if you feel like something a little louder, the adjoining Charlie's Bar is always lively and sociable.

On the Stage

ACROBATICS

The art of acrobatics—the physical feat and spectacle of gymnastic display—was practiced in China over 2,000 years ago and is still going strong. Training academies enroll students of primary school age, and it is not uncommon to see very young children performing alongside seasoned professionals. Each troupe develops its own program, blending vaudeville with gymnastics and acrobatics that require incredible training and concentration.

BEIJING CONCERT HALL

There is nowhere better to appreciate classical Chinese music than in the 1,000-seat Beijing Concert Hall (Beijing Yinyueting), known for its excellent acoustics. Western music is also performed.

✚ F7 ✉ 1 Beixinhua Jie, Xincheng District ☎ 6605 5812; www.artstoday.com 🕐 Evenings ✖ Xidan

CHINA ACROBATIC TROUPE

This remarkable troupe, founded over 40 years ago, offers one of Beijing's more enjoyable evening experiences. The repertoire encompasses plate stacking and spinning, tightrope walking, magic and juggling, interspersed with breathtaking gymnastic displays that are often packed with dramatic surprises involving bicycles or pieces of furniture. Highly recommended.

✚ N5 ✉ Chaoyang Theater, 36 Dongsanhuanbei Lu, Chaoyang District (opposite Jing Guang Hotel) ☎ 6507 2421/1818 🕐 7.15pm 🚍 9, 113, 402, 405, 801

CHINA PUPPETRY THEATER

Chinese shadow puppetry is a dying art, so an opportunity to see a show at the China Puppetry Theater should not be missed, especially if a troupe from the countryside is performing.

✚ Off the map ✉ 1A, Anhuaxili, Chaoyang District (off Beisanhuan Xilu, the Third Ring Road, in the north of the city) ☎ 6425 47998 🕐 Sat 10.30am & 3pm , Sun 3pm 🚍 300, 302

EXPERIMENTAL THEATER FOR MODERN DRAMA

It is only since the death of Mao's fourth wife, an actress and the notorious leader of the Gang of Four, that the authorities have encouraged non-Chinese forms of theater. This is the main venue for such endeavors, and while some shows are in Chinese, international groups also perform in English.

✚ G/H3 ✉ 45A Mao'er Hutong, Xicheng District ☎ 6403 1009/6402 0151 🕐 Evenings 🚍 5, 107, 305

HUAXIA CULTURAL AND MARTIAL ARTS CENTER

Different groups perform here on different nights of the week, perhaps staging a cultural narrative dance, like the traditional Chinese story of the Monkey King, or more often a display of martial arts. The Wushu, a fast and skillful performance of tai chi using swords, is a regular feature of the weekday evening shows and is especially popular.

✚ H6 ✉ National Children's Arts Theater, 64 Dong'anmen Dajie, Dongchen District ☎ 6512 9687 🚍 103, 104

HUGUANG GUILD HALL

Nightly performances of Beijing opera draw the crowds to this theater, which is also the site where Dr. Sun Yat Sen established the Kuomintang in 1912.

✚ F9 ✉ 3 Hufangqiao Lu, Xuanwun District ☎ 6351 8284/6352 9134
🕐 7.15pm–8.45pm
Ⓜ Xuanwumen

LAO SHE TEAHOUSE

The Chinese cultural shows staged here nightly enliven excerpts from Chinese opera with comedy routines (in Chinese but highly visual), martial arts displays, acrobatics, unicycling and magic are also performed.

✚ G7 ✉ 3rd Floor, Da Wan Cha Building, 3 Qianmenxi Dajie, Xuanwu District ☎ 6303 6830
🕐 7.40–9.20 Ⓜ Qianmen

LIYUAN THEATER

The Beijing Opera Troupe performs Chinese opera here daily. Screens alongside the stage carry English translations, and English program notes help you to appreciate what is going on during the show as you sit at the Ming-style tables sipping tea.

✚ F9 ✉ Qianmen Hotel, 175 Yong'an Lu, Xuanwu District ☎ 6301 6688 ext. 8860
🕐 7.30–8.40 Ⓜ Qianmen

PRINCE GONG'S THEATER

See performances of Beijing opera in a beautifully decorated 19th-century private theater (▶ 57). Times vary, but if you sign up for the guided tour of the residence between 8.30am and 4.30pm, it's part of the deal.

✚ G3 ✉ 17 Qianhai Xijie, Xicheng District ☎ 6616 8149

🕐 8.30am–4.30pm 🚌 107, 111, 118

POLY PLAZA INTERNATIONAL THEATER

This is a major venue for ballet, music and opera—Puccini's *Turandot*, the New York City Ballet or the Beijing Jazz Festival.

✚ L4 ✉ 14 Dongzhimennan Dajie, Dongcheng District ☎ 6500 1188 ext. 5126
Ⓜ Dongsishitiao

TIAN QIAO ACROBATICS THEATER

The well-known acrobatic and dance troupe performs in this 100-year-old theater. Possibly less touristy than the shows by the China Acrobatic Troupe in the Chaoyang Theater (▶ 84).

✚ G9 ✉ 95 Tian Qiao Shichang Lu (east end of Beiwei Lu), Xuanwu District ☎ 6303 7449 🕐 Performance 5.30–6.30, 7.15–8.40 🚌 59

ZHENGYICI THEATER

The history of this theater goes back to 1620, when it was first built as a temple. Converted into a hotel after 1949, then finally closed down, it was saved from demolition in 1994 by a millionaire opera aficionado who financed a lavish reconstruction. Today, there is nowhere better to watch Beijing opera. Admission usually includes tea and cookies (during the day, the theater reverts to a teahouse).

✚ F7 ✉ 220 Xiheyan Dajie, Xuanwu District ☎ 6315 1649
🕐 Nightly performances
Ⓜ Xuanwumen

CHINESE OPERA

This highly stylized ancient art form has only a passing resemblance to Western opera and leaves most Westerners utterly bemused. The richly costumed players mix dance and song with mime—accompanied by Chinese instruments. Some grasp of the basic plot will help in understanding the action. The usual five-hour performance is reduced to a mere 90 minutes for the benefit of foreigners, although full performances are rare nowadays. The shortest performances are at the Lao She Teahouse (▶ left).

Luxury Hotels

ROOM PRICES

Approximate prices for a double room, per night:

Luxury	over 1500 yuan
Mid-range	700–1500 yuan
Budget	under 700 yuan

USE YOUR HOTEL

Beijing hotels offer one invaluable service apart from providing a room and shelter: They will write down your destination in Chinese for you to show to taxi drivers when you go out. Ask the doorman to make sure that the driver knows exactly where you want to go—and don't forget to take the hotel's own namecard with you for the return journey.

CHINA WORLD

Consistently one of Beijing's best hotels, with 738 tastefully furnished rooms, superb restaurants and first-class gym, swimming pool and golf center with two golf simulators.

🛇 N7 ✉ 1 Jianguomenwai Dajie, Chaoyang District ☎ 6505 2266, fax 6505 0828; www.shangri-la.com 🚇 1, 4, 37, 52

GREAT WALL SHERATON

In the Sanlitun diplomatic district, a short taxi ride from the city center. This 1,000-room hotel is built around a seven-story atrium loaded with creature comforts to make your stay ultra-luxurious.

🛇 N3 ✉ 10 Dongsanhuanbei Lu, Chaoyang District ☎ 6590 5566, fax 6590 5566; www.sheraton.beijing.com 🚇 300, 402, 801

HILTON

Convenient to the airport and the Sanlitun diplomatic and shopping district. Calm and attractive. 340 rooms

🛇 N2 ✉ 1, Dongfang Lu, Chaoyang District ☎ 6466 2288, fax 6465 3073; www.beijing.hilton.com 🚇 300, 402, 801

NEW CENTURY

Good for families and sports-lovers. The recreation center includes a good-size pool, a bowling alley and outdoor tennis courts. Good transportation to the city center. 720 rooms.

🛇 A3 ✉ Shoudu Tiyuguannan Lu, Haidian District ☎ 6849 2001, fax 6849 1103; www.c-b-w.com/hotel/newcentury 🚇 Xizhimen

PENINSULA PALACE

The Palace vies with China World as Beijing's best hotel and exudes luxury in 511 rooms. Within walking distance of the Forbidden City. Restaurants, pool, health club and dance club.

🛇 J6 ✉ 8 Jinyu Hutong, Dongcheng District ☎ 8516 2888, fax 6510 6311; www.peninsula.com 🚇 103, 11, 106

RADISSON SAS

Terrific rooms (362), a good-size pool, tennis and squash courts and a Finnish sauna help make the Radisson popular, especially with Scandinavians. A large supermarket is next door.

🛇 Just north of M1 ✉ 6A Beisanhuandong Lu, Chaoyang District ☎ 6466 3388, fax 6465 3186; www.radissonsas.com 🚇 302, 18

SWISSOTEL

Few hotels in Beijing have geared themselves so successfully and pleasantly to the needs of Western vacationers. A subway station is nearby and the f454 rooms and facilities are generally excellent, including those for visitors with disabilities. Airport shuttle bus.

🛇 L4 ✉ Hong Kong Macau Center, Gongshi Tiao Lu, Chaoyang District ☎ 6553 2288, fax 6501 2501, www.swissotel.com 🚇 Dongsishitao

Mid-Range Hotels

BAMBOO GARDEN HOTEL

In a quiet lane near the Drum Tower, yet only a 5-minute walk from the subway. Each of the 40 rooms is equipped with satellite TV but if you are to enjoy your stay you must have a balcony overlooking the garden.

✚ G2 ✉ 24 Xiaoshiqiao Hutong (off Jiugulou Dajie), Xicheng District ☎ 6512 8833, fax 6401 2633; www.bbgh.com.cn 🚇 Gulou Dajie

HOLIDAY INN DOWNTOWN

Conveniently close to a subway station and shopping malls. It has a good recreation center, an affordable Western-style restaurant and 347 rooms.

✚ D4 ✉ 98 Beilishi Lu, Xicheng District ☎ 6833 8822, fax 6834 0696 🚇 Fuchengmen

JIANGUO HOTEL QIANMEN

Not too far from the Forbidden City, the refurbished Qianmen has 400 rooms, a chic lobby, good restaurants, a gym, sauna and billiard room. Rates are at the lower end of the price category but large groups of mainland tourists stay here.

✚ F9 ✉ 175 Yong'an Lu, Xuanwu District ☎ 6301 6688, fax 6301 3883 🚌 15, 25, 102

MINZU

A good hotel in a useful location just west of the city center. The 607 rooms are pleasantly decorated. It also boasts a gym and a billiards room.

✚ E7 ✉ 51 Fuxingmennei

Dajie, Xicheng District ☎ 6601 4466, fax 6601 4849 🚇 Xidan

OCEAN

In an up-and-coming commercial area whose nightclubs come alive with neon at night, this smart modern 70-room hotel is within walking distance of the Forbidden City.

✚ J6 ✉ 189 Dongsinan Jie, Dongcheng District ☎ 6522 8888, fax 6522 9564 🚌 110, 116

NOVOTEL PEACE

This hotel, at the top end of the price range, is in the heart of the city, with 337 rooms, indoor pool and restaurants.

✚ J6 ✉ 3 Jinyu Hutong, Dongcheng District ☎ 6512 8833, fax 6512 6863 🚌 104, 111

SONGHE

The Songhe is well versed in the art of dealing with Western visitors and conveniently close to Wangfujing Dajie and the Forbidden City. The 310 rooms are at the top end of the category.

✚ J5 ✉ 88 Dengshikou Dajie, Dongcheng District ☎ 6513 8822, fax 6513 9088 🚌 111, 108

XINDADU

Also called the Beijing Mandarin, this elegant four-star hotel is in the northwest of the city, south of the zoo. It has 530 rooms, a swimming pool, a sauna and fitness center and several restaurants.

✚ B4 ✉ 21 Chegongzhuangxi Lu, Xicheng District ☎ 6831 9988, fax 6833 8507 🚇 Xizhimen

REST ASSURED

The days when hotel staff strolled into hotel rooms uninvited are long gone. The general standard of hotels that welcome foreign guests is high. When you choose accommodations in Beijing today, a hotel's location and availability of transportation to the city center are usually the most relevant considerations. (Apart from the Xindadu, all the hotels on this spread are close to the city center.)

Budget Accommodations

WORTH CONSIDERING

Backpackers favor the Jinghua Hotel (☎ 6722 2211) on Nansanhuan Zhong Lu for its budget dormitory accommodations, inexpensive restaurants, economically priced tours to the Great Wall, bicycle rental facility, and general willingness to provide information. The big drawback is its location, on the southern end of the Third Ring Road. Take bus 17 from Qianmen to the Haihutun bus station and walk from there.

BEIJING LIEN HOTEL

Downtown budget hotel with clean rooms, color television, private baths and all upscale amenities at a fraction of a luxury price.
✚ L4 ✉ 3 Xinzhong Xi Jie, Goungti Bei Lu (off East 2nd Ring Road) ☎ 6553 1503
🚇 Dong Si Shi Tiao

BULLION KAI YUE HOTEL

Modern 3-star hotel (opened 2004) with excellent facilities and only a few minutes' walk from the shopping malls and boutiques of Wangfujing Dajie and Sun Dong An Market. All 108 rooms are comfortable, clean and great value.
✚ J6 ✉ 31 Ganyu Hutong, Wangfujing Dajie, Dongcheng District ☎ 8511 0388, fax 6528 1028 🚇 Wangfujing

DONG FANG

Value hotel with good facilities. In the Qianmen area, the Dong Fang has eight restaurants, a sauna, gym, business center and a laundry. All 320 rooms are air-conditioned.
✚ F9 ✉ 11 Wanming Lu, Xuanwu District ☎ 6301 4466, fax 6304 4801 🚌 59, 105

FANGYAN

Tucked away down a street off Wangfujing. Its 50 rooms are rather drab but good value because it is so central.
✚ H5 ✉ 36 Dengshikouxi Jie, Dongcheng District ☎ 6525 6311, fax 6513 8549
🚌 103, 104, 111

FAR EAST HOTEL

Affordable rooms (78) in the heart of the Dazhalan area, within walking distance of Tian'anmen Square. There is a Chinese restaurant.
✚ F8 ✉ 90 Tieshuxie Jie, Xuanwu District ☎ 6301 8811, fax 6301 8233 🚇 Qianmen

GUOZHAN

This modern hotel is an affordable option for anyone seeking budget accommodations within reach of good food—the Royal Café of the Radisson SAS Hotel (▶ 71) and a huge supermarket are across the street. The hotel has 70 standard rooms with air-conditioning and a Sichuan restaurant.
✚ Just north of M1 ✉ 10 Jianga Xi Lu, Chaoyang District ☎ 6463 9922, fax 6467 9040 🚌 302, 379

LUSONGYUAN

This is a charming, traditional choice, if a little out of the way—about 4 miles (7km) from Tian'anmen Square. It is styled like the surrounding historic buildings with multiple courtyards and pagoda-style roofs. Despite appearances, it has an up-to-date business center and internet access.
✚ Off map ✉ 22 Banchang Lane, Kuanjie ☎ 6404 0436, fax 6403 0418

RAINBOW

A decent modern 300-room Chinese hotel, with few foreign visitors and little English spoken, in the interesting Qianmen area.
✚ F9 ✉ 11 Xijing Lu, Xuanwu District ☎ 6301 2266, fax 6301 1366 🚌 59, 106, 343

BEIJING
travel facts

ESSENTIAL FACTS

Electricity

- The supply is 220 volts, 50 cycles AC current. Sockets come in a variety of sizes and types. Big hotels can supply adaptors, but it is best to bring your own.

Etiquette

- Confrontation or a public display of anger is counter-productive.
- Other public displays of strong emotion are not advisable.
- Avoid discussing Chinese politics.

Money matters

- Most major credit cards are accepted at hotels, and at an increasing number of smarter restaurants and stores.
- Travelers' checks (in dollars) are safer than cash and attract a better exchange rate. They can be cashed at the Bank of China and at bureaux de change.
- If prices are not displayed, polite bargaining is probably expected.

National holidays

- 1 Jan (New Year's Day)
- Chinese New Year/Spring Festival.
- 8 Mar (International Working Women's Day)
- 1 May (International Labor Day)
- 4 May (Youth Day)
- 1 Jun (Children's Day)
- 1 Jul (Anniversary of Founding of Communist Party of China)
- 1 Aug (Anniversary of Founding of the PLA)
- 1 Oct (National Day)

Opening hours

- Banks and offices: Mon–Fri 9–5.
- Stores: Generally 9–6, often later.

Places of worship

- Foreigners are free to attend services in the city:
- Catholic: St. Mary's Church Nantang Cathedral (Southern Cathedral) ✉ 141 Qianmenxi Dajie, Xuanwu District ☎ 6602 5221
- Protestant: Beitang/Northern Cathedral ✉ 33 Xishiku Dajie, Xicheng District ☎ 6617 5198
- Church of Jesus Christ of Latter-Day Saints ✉ Capital Mansions, 4th Floor, 6 Xinyuannan Lu, Chaoyang District ☎ 6532 4251
- Judaism: Weekly Sabbath services ✉ Capital Mansions, 3rd Floor, Capital Club Athletic Center, 6 Xinyuannan Lu, Chaoyang District ☎ 6512 6662/6505 3701

Student travelers

- Very few discounts are available.

Tipping

- Tipping is not routinely expected, except for guides.

Toilets

- Hotels and better restaurants have Western-style toilets. Elsewhere expect hole-in-the-ground toilets. Outside better hotels and restaurants, standards of cleanliness are not always good.

Tourist offices

- There is no tourist information office but a tourist hotline ☎ 6513 0828 is available. Hotel staff are usually helpful.

GETTING AROUND

How to use the subway

- There are two main lines. On western maps the main circle line is called the loop, which, runs beneath the Second Ring Road. The second line, runs west–east across the city via Tian'anmen Square. A short walk is necessary to connect from one line to the other.

- Most station names are in English. The only problem you may have is trying to figure out in which direction a train is heading when it pulls into the station.

How to use the buses

- There is a confusing array of vehicles: red and white, blue and white, trolley-buses, double-decker buses, and private minibuses that carry the same number as the bus route they follow. On minibuses, you can always get a seat, and the vehicle will stop anywhere along the route. Public buses are often very crowded in contrast and only the air-conditioned ones—like bus 801, which runs between the Lufthansa Center (➕ N2) and the junction with Jianguomenwai Dajie (➕ N7)—offer any comfort.
- Know your destination stop in Chinese.

Where to get maps

- Foreign Languages Bookstore (➤ 79) and some hotel stores sell a Chinese/English city map that shows all the bus routes.

Types of ticket

- Subway tickets cost 3 yuan regardless of the length of the journey. You hand it to an attendant upon going downstairs to the platform.
- Bus tickets are calculated according to the length of the journey. The basic fare is 1 yuan and longer journeys cost 2 yuan. Tickets are purchased from the conductor, but often the buses are so crowded that you have difficulty even seeing him. Fares on minibuses range between 2 and 6 yuan depending on length of journey.

Taxis

- The price rates for taxis depend on the make of the cab. The most common, Xialis, charge 10 yuan for the first 2.5 miles (4km), then 1.2 yuan per half mile (1km). Sedans cost 1.6 yuan per half mile and the first 2 miles (3km). The luxurious but rare VW Sanatans start at 12 yuan and increase at 2 yuan per half mile after 2 miles (3km). Cab fares are expected to rise following major fuel price hikes, while the cab fleet will be modernized in time for the Olympics in 2008. Between 11pm and 6am, a 20 percent surcharge is added.
- Always ask someone at your hotel to write down your destination in Chinese and show this to the driver before setting off.

MEDIA & COMMUNICATIONS

Sending letters and packages

- The easiest way to send letters and postcards is from your hotel.
- Sending packages is time-consuming and often frustrating since printed matter has to be wrapped by postal officials. Leave parcels open because they must be inspected at the post office.
- Smaller packages can be sent from most post offices. Larger parcels need to go from the main post office: the International Post Office (➕ L6 ✉ Jianguomenwai Dajie ☎ 6512 8120).

Telephones

- Local calls are free, and hotels usually only charge a nominal fee.
- The easiest and least expensive way to make an international call is to use a card telephone in a hotel. Cards come in denominations of 100 yuan and may be purchased

from hotel shops and hotel business centers.

- Use business centers in hotels to send faxes and emails. It does not matter if you are not a guest.

Newspapers and magazines

- The only Chinese newspaper in English is the *China Daily*, which carries listings on Fridays.
- The *International Herald Tribune*, *Asian Wall Street Journal* and the Hong Kong-produced *South China Morning Post* are also in English.
- *Time*, *Newsweek*, *Far Eastern Economic Review*, and *The Economist* are sold in a few hotel shops. French and German magazines are available in some top-class hotels.
- *Beijing This Month*, *City Weekend* and *That's Beijing* have listings.

Television

- Better hotels carry CNN and Star TV from Hong Kong.
- The *China Daily* lists times of the English-language news broadcasts on state television channels.

EMERGENCIES

Emergency phone numbers

- Police 110. Ambulance 120. Fire 119. (Chinese only.)

Embassies and consulates

- Australia ✉ 21 Dongzhimenwai Dajie ☎ 6532 2331–7
- Canada ✉ 19 Dongzhimenwai Dajie ☎ 6532 3536
- France ✉ 13 Dongsanjie, Sanlitun ☎ 6532 1331
- Germany ✉ 17 Dongzhimenwai Dajie ☎ 6532 2161
- Ireland ✉ 3 Ritan Donglu ☎ 6532 2914
- Italy ✉ 2 Dong'erjie, Sanlitun ☎ 6532 2131
- New Zealand ✉ 1 Ritan Lu Dong'erjie, Jianguomenwai, Chaoyang District ☎ 6532 2731–3

- UK ✉ 11 Guanghua Lu ☎ 5192 4000. Visa and consular services ✉ 21st floor Kerry Center, I Guanghua Lu ☎ 8529 6600
- USA ✉ 3 Xishui Beijie, Jianguomenwai Dajie ☎ 6532 3831, ext. 209 for consular services

Medical treatment

- Better hotels have their own medical services. Clinics with English-speaking staff include:
- Hong Kong International Medical Clinic ✉ Swissotel (Hong Kong Macau Center), Dongsi Tiao Lu, Chaoyang District ☎ 6501 4260 (24hr: 6553 2288, ext 2346)
- International Medical Center ✉ Lufthansa Center, Regus Office Building, Room 106, 50 Liangmaqiao Lu, Chaoyang District ☎ 6465 1561
- Sino-Japanese Friendship Hospital ✉ Yinghua Donglu, Hepingli Beikou ☎ 6422 1122 ext. 3411

Medicines

- Stores in top-class hotels often sell simple medicines—most notably the Watsons store at the Holiday Inn Lido (outside the city center, towards the airport). Some bigger supermarkets, like those in the Lufthansa Center and the China World Trade Shopping Center (► 78), are also worth trying. The International Medical Center has a pharmacy.

Sensible precautions

- Beijing is generally very safe.
- Pickpockets operate in crowded places like rail stations and on buses; secure all belongings.
- Leave money and important documents in your hotel room safe or safety-deposit box.
- Always keep travelers' checks separate from your record of their numbers, and note the emergency contact number in case of loss.
- Bring a photocopy of your passport and visa in case of theft.

LANGUAGE

- In general, the better the hotel the better the standard of English spoken and understood. On the street, you cannot rely on communicating in any language other than Chinese. Although many people know some English, it is useful (as well as courteous) to know some basic spoken Chinese.

- The modern phonetic romanized form of Chinese is called "pinyin." It is largely pronounced as written, but note the following:

  a as in c*a*r

  c as in bi*ts* as an initial consonant

  e as in h*e*r

  i as in f*ee*t unless preceded by c, ch, r, s, sh, z, sh, when it becomes *er* as in her

  j as in *g*in

  o as in f*o*rd

  q like the ch in *ch*in

  s as in *s*imple

  u as in oo in c*oo*l

  w as in *w*ade, though pronounced by some as v

  x like the sh in *sh*eep but with the s given greater emphasis

  y as in *yo*yo

  z as ds in li*ds*; zh as j in jam

Basics

yes	shi
no	bu shi
I don't understand	bu dong
Do you understand?	Dong ma?
when?	shenme shi hou?
where?	nar?
telephone	dianhua
police	jingcha
toilet	ce suo
excuse me	dui bu qi
time	shijian
doctor	yi sheng
hospital	yiyuan
pharmacy	yaodian

Greetings, etc.

hello/how are you?	ni hao
please	qing
thank you	xiexie
goodbye	zai jian
My surname is…	Wo xing…
I am from	Who shi…laide

Getting around

Where is…?	…zai nali?
taxi	chuzu che
airport	fei ji chang
train	huoche
bus	gong gong qi che
bicycle	xi xing che
ticket	piao
turn right	You zhuan
turn left	Zuo zhuan
I'm lost	Wo milule
hotel	fandian
room	fang jian
post office	youju
bank	yin hang

Shopping

how much?	Duo shao qian?
too expensive	tai gui le
a little cheaper	pian yi dian ba
gift	li wu
credit card	xin yong ka
postcards	ming xin pian
stamps	you piao
antique	guwu
silk	sichou
rice	mifan
beer	pijiu
coffee	ka fei

Numbers

0	ling	9	jiu
1	yi, yao	10	shi
2	er, liang	11	shiyi
3	san	12	shier
4	si	20	ershi
5	wu	21	ershiyi
6	liu	100	yibai
7	qi	200	erbai
8	ba	1,000	yiqian

93

Index